Inside
and Out

Inside
and Out

Living Like Jesus
in Today's World

NICKI DECHERT CARLSON

XULON ELITE

Xulon Press Elite
555 Winderley Pl, Suite 225
Maitland, FL 32751
407.339.4217
www.xulonpress.com

Paperback ISBN-13: 978-1-66289-760-3
Ebook ISBN-13: 978-1-66289-761-0

Contents

... and Out

for Kristi

May you experience the love of Christ, though it is too great to understand fully. Then you will be made complete with all the fullness of life and power that comes from God.

(Ephesians 3:19)

Preface

Jesus amazes me. I adore Him. I love studying His interactions with ordinary people like you and me. No one ever encountered Jesus without being changed for the better. This causes me to wonder why so many people feel deeply hurt today by the contemporary Christian church. Most people left Jesus's presence feeling better, not worse. If we can't say the same about our churches today, what are we doing wrong?

I decided to study Jesus's earthly ministry for answers, and I became convinced that if we are to create the change we want to see in our world and our churches, we need to look and act a lot more like Jesus. Instead of asking what Jesus would do, let's take a look at what Jesus already did and learn from that. Jesus didn't come to earth solely to die for us; He also came to show us how to live.

The more I learn, the more I realize I understand and know so little. I do not have all the answers. One thing I do know is that it's not possible to live entirely like Jesus because He was divine, and we are not. We can strive to live a little *more* like Jesus day by day, though—by studying Him, applying His teachings, and through the in-dwelling help of the Holy Spirit. I pray this book helps us do exactly that.

I feel overwhelmingly humbled to put this book into your hands . . . humbled God chose to teach me about His Son, humbled by the example of Jesus, humbled by the opportunity to share these words with you, and humbled at the feet of a savior who has shown me His endless grace and mercy, time and time again. I often feel unworthy to share this message, because who am I to teach anyone how to live like our Lord? However, God gently reminds me of the people Jesus chose to work with during His time on earth. He did not seek out the near-perfect or the religious experts, but everyday people like you and me, struggling through life.

I must tell you, I'm just an imperfect person talking about a perfect God. I'm a woman trying to find God in everyday life and live out my love for Jesus.

If we want to make the world a better place, I believe it starts right here with Jesus. I am so happy you are joining me on this journey to live more like Him, inside and out. I'm excited to see where it takes us.

Introduction

> Christ is the visible image of the invisible God. He existed before anything was created and is supreme over all creation, for through him God created everything in the heavenly realms and on earth. He made the things we can see and the things we can't see—such as thrones, kingdoms, rulers, and authorities in the unseen world. Everything was created through him and for him.
>
> (Colossians 1:15–16)

From the beginning, there was God, Jesus (His Son), and the Holy Spirit. God created humans, and in the garden of Eden, Adam and Eve sinned and broke intimate fellowship with their perfect Creator, God. The Bible tells the story of a benevolent God who gradually discloses more of Himself to His people to draw them back into a flawless and complete relationship with Him, similar to the one Adam and Eve had in the garden before their transgression. Jesus was God's ultimate weapon for doing this. Jesus restored the broken connection between humanity and God through the blood sacrifice of His own life. Christ is timeless: He was present in the beginning, He lived on the earth, He resides now in heaven, and He will return to the earth again in final victory.

God chose to reveal Himself through Jesus Christ wholly. It's difficult for us to imagine who God is, what He looks like, or how His personality might appear. When we try to simplify who and what God is, we run the risk of excluding entire facets of His character. We can, however, look to Jesus—God in the flesh—and His life and ministry on earth for answers.

Who is Jesus? He is the one who stays when everyone else walks away. He loves the unlovable. He forgives the unforgivable. He comforts the inconsolable. He finds the lost. He cures the sick. He heals the broken. He saves the unsalvageable. He communes with sinners. He includes the outcasts. He offers grace and mercy to the guilty. He serves even though He is the Lord. He turns an upside-down kingdom right-side-up again. Jesus is relationship over legalism, honesty without condemnation, power without abuse, wisdom without pride, strength without intimidation, and humility without timidity.

> *Jesus is relationship over legalism, honesty without condemnation, power without abuse, wisdom without pride, strength without intimidation, and humility without timidity.*

If we want to know God so we can please Him and be in communion with Him, we can imitate the most accurate reflection of who He is: Jesus Christ. We can strive to think, speak, and act like Jesus did while He walked the earth. He's been here and seen it all. He is the guide we seek for knowing and understanding the God who created us.

> For the law was given through Moses, but God's unfailing love and faithfulness came through Jesus Christ. No one has ever seen God. But the unique One,

who is himself God, is near to the Father's heart. He has revealed God to us.

(John 1:17–18)

We have no better method for getting to know our Heavenly Father than getting to know His Son. Jesus reveals God's "unfailing love and faithfulness." Jesus says if we know Him, then we already know the Father. He came to teach us who God is by showing us what God looks like in real life.

> Philip said, "Lord, show us the Father, and we will be satisfied."
>
> Jesus replied, "Have I been with you all this time, Philip, and yet you still don't know who I am? Anyone who has seen me has seen the Father! So why are you asking me to show him to you? Don't you believe that I am in the Father and the Father is in me? The words I speak are not my own, but my Father who lives in me does his work through me. Just believe that I am in the Father and the Father is in me. Or at least believe because of the work you have seen me do.
>
> I tell you the truth, anyone who believes in me will do the same works I have done, and even greater works, because I am going to be with the Father."
>
> (John 14:8–12)

Despite having a divine nature that we do not, Jesus says we "will do the same works He has done, indeed, even greater works" than Him. We're not just saved *because* of Jesus; we're saved *by* Jesus. We don't just get to *see* Jesus at work in the world; we get to *join* Jesus in His work in the world. He isn't some cold, distant deity. Jesus calls us His brothers, sisters, and friends. Our Savior is personal because He chose to empty Himself of His divine privilege and become one of us. He experienced hunger, thirst, disappointment, grief, anger, loneliness, abandonment, and more . . . just like we do. He knew joy, thanksgiving, creativity, and laughter. He knows us inside and out.

But just how will we ordinary humans do "even greater works" than Jesus? Consider the fact that Jesus was only one man. We Christians, however, number in the billions. What would it look like if we all internalized the character of Jesus and lived it out in the world? What if, for example, we forgave others like Jesus? What if we drew near to those in need like Jesus? What if we worshiped, prayed, and taught like Jesus? In other words, *what if we lived like Jesus, inside and out*?

The apostle Paul attempted to describe, in His letter to the Philippians, how this might look in practice.

> Is there any encouragement from belonging to Christ? Any comfort from his love? Any fellowship together in the Spirit? Are your hearts tender and compassionate? Then make me truly happy by agreeing wholeheartedly with each other, loving one another, and working together with one mind and purpose. Don't be selfish; don't try to impress others. Be humble, thinking of others as better than yourselves. Don't look out only for your own interests, but take an interest in others, too.
>
> You must have the same attitude that Christ Jesus had. Though he was God, he did not think of equality with God as something to cling to. Instead, he gave up his divine privileges; he took the humble position of a slave

and was born as a human being. When he appeared in
human form, he humbled himself in obedience to God
and died a criminal's death on a cross.

(Philippians 2:1–8)

Paul says we are to offer fellowship and compassion, encourage,
comfort, love, work together, show generosity and humility, look
out for others, and be obedient to God
. . . just to name a few ways we can strive
to live like Jesus. We must cultivate the
mind of Christ inside, so we can model
the behavior of Christ on the outside.

> *We must cultivate
> the mind of Christ
> inside, so we can
> model the behavior
> of Christ on
> the outside.*

We know from biblical stories that
Paul sought to imitate Christ, including
performing miracles in His name. A
story in the book of Acts tells of how
Paul brought a young man named Eutychus back from the dead.
Referencing this story, biblical scholar and author Kristi McLelland
says Paul "knew that following Jesus was not just knowing what
Jesus knew, but being like Him."[1] In other words, Paul knew it was
not enough just to *know* Jesus. It was not enough just to *believe* in
Jesus. Paul knew he needed to *live*—to think, speak, behave, react,
lead, and teach—just like Jesus did.

It begs the question: Is Jesus Christ truly our Lord, or is He
merely a hobby or an interest? Does Jesus infiltrate every aspect of
our lives, or do we simply have occasional experiences with Him?
Do we daily and actively try to think and behave as He would, or
do we prioritize our own comfort and pleasure instead?

Jesus asks a very direct question of us in the sixth chapter of
Luke.

"So why do you keep calling me 'Lord, Lord!' when you don't do what I say?"

(Luke 6:46)

If we claim to follow Jesus, then our lives should look like His. Our attitude should resemble His. If we want Jesus to be the Lord of our lives, we must get off His throne. We must center our lives on Christ alone and live according to His example.

It's not enough for us to simply *know* Jesus. We must *live* like Jesus, inside and out.

Live Like Jesus on the *Inside*

The more time we spend studying the Word of God and the life of Jesus, the more open and available we become to Him. Jesus will seize this opportunity to transform us more and more into His likeness. If we want to live like Jesus, we must internalize His character and learn to think and feel as He does.

Heaven, Traffic Light Elves, and Other Things We Don't Understand

—— *Hope like Jesus* ——

"Mom, are the people that push the buttons for the lights there at night?" my five-year-old asked as we drove down the street.

"What are you talking about, Sweetie?" I inquired.

"*Those* lights!" he exclaimed, pointing to the traffic lights. "Where do the people that live inside the lights go at night?" Frustrated by my confusion, he continued, "You knooooow . . . the little people that push the button inside to make it red, green, or yellow?" he asked impatiently.

"Johnathan, those lights work all by themselves. There are no little people in there," I answered.

"Yes there arrrrre!" he whined, clearly disappointed with my answer.

"Well, if there are, then I guess they go to bed at eight o'clock, just like you. Don't worry. You're not missing anything exciting," I explained, hoping to resolve the issue.

Children make up all kinds of interesting explanations for things they can't understand. Honestly, we adults do, too. Take the matter of heaven, for example. Ask any five people to describe heaven and you will undoubtedly receive five completely different answers. Despite the discrepancies, heaven still sounds pretty great. I often say I can't wait to get there. The truth is, though, I *can* wait. Why? Because I know God isn't calling me home just yet. This raises the question of how we should balance the challenges of our everyday lives with the hope of a paradise in the future. How do we keep one foot on the ground while metaphorically climbing the stairs to heaven?

Pastor David Payne says, "The goal isn't to get to heaven. The goal is to bring heaven to earth." This statement blew my mind the first time I heard it. Suddenly, I realized the importance of being a missionary for Christ, every day. My job is to help turn my tiny corner of the world into a new holy utopia, a new garden of Eden, and a new heaven-on-earth.

We lost paradise on earth when Adam and Eve rebelled and sinned against God in the garden of Eden. Sin entered the world, and perfection fell instantly into imperfection. We can trace all the suffering and gradual decay of our world and our bodies to that first fall from grace. We cry out in agony as we ache desperately for the return to the purity and ideal of the garden, where humans enjoyed perfect communion with God while walking the earth. That "return" comes when Christ returns to earth for final victory, or when our souls return to heaven where we will once again enjoy untarnished fellowship with our Father.

The human part of Jesus had to feel this same desperate longing while He walked the earth. He was also divine, after all; He *remembered* heaven. So, Christ lived with a particular hope—a hope of His resurrection and return to glory. He explained this to His disciples.

> "Listen," he said, "we're going up to Jerusalem, where the Son of Man will be betrayed to the leading priests and

the teachers of religious law. They will sentence him to die and hand him over to the Romans. They will mock him, spit on him, flog him with a whip, and kill him, but after three days he will rise again."

(Mark 10:33–34)

"I brought glory to you here on earth by completing the work you gave me to do. Now, Father, bring me into the glory we shared before the world began."

(John 17:4–5)

In the Old Testament, hope referred to expectation and an unwavering trust in God. The New Testament adds to this definition by explaining we find our hope in our Savior, Jesus. Evangelist Billy Graham said, "For the believer there is hope beyond the grave because Jesus Christ has opened the door to heaven for us by His death and resurrection."[2] He is our only chance at heaven. He is the offering of atonement for our sins. He is our only hope.

Praise be to the God and Father of our Lord Jesus Christ! In his great mercy he has given us new birth into a living hope through the resurrection of Jesus Christ from the dead, and into an inheritance that can never perish, spoil or fade. This inheritance is kept in heaven for you, who through faith are shielded by God's power until the coming of the salvation that is ready to be revealed in the last time.

(1 Peter 1:3–5 NIV)

Jesus is our hope for eternity and, according to this verse, that hope cannot be taken from us. It resides inside of us in this present day, prompting us to live our lives differently . . . more like He led His. With our eyes trained on the sacrifice of Jesus and an eternal future with Him in paradise, the difficulties this life presents lose some of their urgency and dominion over us.

> We can rejoice, too, when we run into problems and trials, for we know that they help us develop endurance. And endurance develops strength of character, and character strengthens our confident hope of salvation. And this hope will not lead to disappointment. For we know how dearly God loves us, because he has given us the Holy Spirit to fill our hearts with his love.
>
> (Romans 5:3–5)

In addition to navigating trials, we must also take care to balance our hope of heaven with our mission here in the world, because the two concepts go hand-in-hand. Remember, the goal isn't gaining heaven for ourselves, but bringing heaven down to earth. We must be obedient to God's callings on our lives to serve Him, to serve others, and to worship Him.

> Let us hold tightly without wavering to the hope we affirm, for God can be trusted to keep his promise. Let us think of ways to motivate one another to acts of love and good works. And let us not neglect our meeting together, as some people do, but encourage one another, especially now that the day of his return is drawing near.
>
> (Hebrews 10:23–25)

Henri Nouwen, the great writer and theologian said, "While optimism makes us live as if someday soon things will get better for us, hope frees us from the need to predict the future and allows us to live in the present, with deep trust God will never leave us alone but will fulfill the deepest desires of our heart. . . . Joy in this perspective is the fruit of hope."[3]

Living in the present while tapping into the joy of our future in heaven is key to navigating this mystery called hope. We trust. We expect. We busy ourselves with the work our Heavenly Father has given us to do here . . . work that brings a little heaven down to earth. This work probably won't look like living inside a traffic signal, pushing tiny buttons to make the lights outside change from red to green. Rest assured that God has gifted each of us with unique tools for doing specific work for Him, though. And we will go about this kingdom work while carrying the hope of heaven inside of us, just like Jesus did.

> *Living in the present while tapping into the joy of our future in heaven is key to navigating this mystery called hope.*

LIVE LIKE JESUS

Inside . . .

Take an honest inventory of your life. Where do you place your hope—in others, your finances, your abilities, or in Jesus?

. . . and Out

Start a journal. Every day, write down at least one example of God's faithfulness. As you record God's provision and faithfulness, you will learn to place your hope and trust in Him, just like Jesus did.

Coffee Beans and Jars of Clay

—— Submit like Jesus ——

I looked out the window with groggy eyes and heard the familiar "whoosh" as the last of the water filtered through the coffee maker. I pulled the filter out and noticed a lone, whole coffee bean sitting precariously on top of the black, soggy mess of coffee grounds. It reminded me that the steaming, liquid goodness I was about to drink at one time held only potential, trapped within the confines of this tiny, hard-shelled bean. We all know the process those beans endure before they render that delicious coffee elixir: planting, watering, weeding, weathering storms, harvesting, transporting, manufacturing, inspecting, packaging, and more transporting. Only after all this do we bring the beans into our homes, put them through a metal grinder, and pour boiling water on top of their remains. Sounds rather violent, does it not?

The journey from a simple coffee bean into a great cup of joe serves as a perfect metaphor for our own journeys—from weak, simple humans into unlikely world changers—when we submit to God's plans for our lives. God spoke this same message to the prophet Jeremiah in a potter's shop, where God had asked Jeremiah to go so He could speak to him.

> So I did as he told me and found the potter working at
> his wheel. But the jar he was making did not turn out as

he had hoped, so he crushed it into a lump of clay again and started over.

Then the LORD gave me this message: "O Israel, can I not do to you as this potter has done to his clay? As the clay is in the potter's hand, so are you in my hand."

(Jeremiah 18:3–6)

I love the image of God poised at the potter's wheel, spinning and shaping, His hands wet and covered in clay, tenderly and systematically working the material until it begins to resemble the vision in His mind. I often feel like I am that clay, with God continuously working on me as He teaches me more and more about Himself until I begin to more closely resemble the ideal "me" He envisions. At times I also feel that painful moment of starting over, when God keeps the potter's wheel spinning, but slows it down and returns my clay form to a shapeless lump to start the process over again. Sometimes God has to tear us down before He can rebuild us into something stronger and more beautiful.

Sometimes God has to tear us down before He can rebuild us into something stronger and more beautiful.

This creative process can prove quite painful, but there's good news. Paul says God will remain faithful and true throughout this entire endeavor.

And I am certain that God, who began the good work within you, will continue his work until it is finally finished on the day when Christ Jesus returns.

(Philippians 1:6)

14

God's pursuit of a relationship with us, His intimacy with us, and His creative process with us doesn't end until the day Christ returns. In the meantime, He will never look at His clay masterpiece-in-the-making, throw up His hands, stop the wheel, and say, "Well, I just can't work with you. I give up." He always sees us—His beloved children—just as we are, while simultaneously seeing our potential. He also sees that, sometimes, we need the pain and suffering of the re-making process to reach our ideal form. In other words, God wants us to yield to His leadership, because when we don't follow His guidance and creative process, we hinder His purposes.

Thankfully, we serve a savior who modeled this kind of submission for us incredibly well. That's right—our God-in-human-form submitted to authorities beyond Himself. For one, we see Jesus yielding to parental authority, when He performed His first miracle at the request of His mother. While attending a wedding in Cana, Jesus's mother realized the family's humiliating mistake: they'd run out of wine. In a Middle Eastern culture, such an occurrence could ruin the family's honor and standing in the community.

> The wine supply ran out during the festivities, so Jesus' mother told him, "They have no more wine."
>
> "Dear woman, that's not our problem," Jesus replied. "My time has not yet come."
>
> But his mother told the servants, "Do whatever he tells you."
>
> (John 2:3–5)

After this mother-son exchange, Jesus turned jars of water into wine, thus saving the family's reputation. Although Jesus initially said, "My time has not yet come," He took His mother's request into account and acquiesced to her wishes.

We also see an example in Scripture of Jesus submitting to a government authority when a group of Pharisees attempted to trap Jesus into saying something that could result in His arrest.

> "Now tell us what you think about this: Is it right to pay taxes to Caesar or not?"
>
> But Jesus knew their evil motives. "You hypocrites!" he said. "Why are you trying to trap me? Here, show me the coin used for the tax." When they handed him a Roman coin, he asked, "Whose picture and title are stamped on it?"
>
> "Caesar's," they replied.
>
> "Well, then," he said, "give to Caesar what belongs to Caesar, and give to God what belongs to God."
>
> (Matthew 22:17–21)

Jesus, the divine, still instructed others to submit to the established government authorities as well as to God, and we know the cost of His submission. Jesus suffered perhaps more than any other being on earth ever has, and He did it for our sake—to accomplish the merciful and grace-filled will of God.

Surrendering to God's will meant Jesus had to endure gross suffering before He could reach His full potential and purpose. Just for a moment, try to imagine Jesus without the agony of the cross. He taught, He healed, He befriended, He led, He challenged—all wonderful, important, life-changing activities. But if there were no cross—no piercing cries of agony, no spectacle of unjust torture, no pleas for forgiveness for His crucifiers, no humble obedience to God's will for Him—He never would have met His full potential of world-changing salvation. Without the cross, there's no mind-bending display of God's power and authority over death. Without the cross, there's no blood sacrifice to allow us to commune with a holy God while still living in our filthy human bodies. Without the cross, there's no redemption, forgiveness, or salvation. Without the cross, there's no Easter. No obedience from Jesus means no resurrection, and no resurrection means no salvation for any of us.

God can make extraordinary things happen with our ordinary surrender.

God has blessed us with the knowledge of Christ and His victory over evil. Because of this knowledge, we now understand the potential found in submitting to God's will. God can make extraordinary things happen with our ordinary surrender. We may be earthen, shatter-prone pottery, but we possess within us the same power that brought Jesus back from the dead. Through the power of submitting to God, we can pass His love, power, and mercy into the world.

> May you experience the love of Christ, though it is too great to understand fully. Then you will be made complete with all the fullness of life and power that comes from God. Now all glory to God, who is able, through his mighty power at work within us, to accomplish infinitely more than we might ask or think.
>
> (Ephesians 3:19–20)

The process of becoming moldable and pliable in our Father's hands isn't always easy or pleasant, and submission may not come naturally to all of us. We don't face this journey alone though, because Jesus walks right alongside us every step of the way. At times, we must endure the bean grinder and the boiling water, or the smashing of the clay on the potter's wheel, so God can release something magnificent lying dormant inside us—our full potential in Him.

LIVE LIKE JESUS

Inside . . .

What keeps you from fully submitting to God's will—from surrendering yourself completely to Him? Is it fear, doubt, bitterness, unforgiveness towards God, or something else? Remember that even Jesus, the son of God, submitted Himself to our Heavenly Father.

. . . and Out

We all struggle to relinquish certain areas of our lives to God's complete control. Spend some time praying about your reluctance to submit fully to God. Ask Him to help you surrender anything to which you may be clinging too tightly and to give you the faith and courage you need to submit yourself completely to His will and His purposes.

Sinking Still

—— *Draw Near like Jesus* ——

I don't even have to close my eyes to transport myself back to this particular moment: the slight taste of salt on my lips, carried by the mist . . . the way my long hair whipped across my face in the breeze . . . the loud call of the seagull flying left to right above my head . . . the rhythmic sound of the waves crashing . . . the warmth of the sun on my bronzed skin. I felt the hot, sugary sand under my bare feet, and I inched forward until the blistering, dry sand turned to cool, wet compacted sand. The remnants of a gentle wave licked my toes and then scurried back to its sea-mother. My feet made prints where I'd stood motionless in the sand. Another wave encroached and covered the tops of my feet and, as it slid backward toward the great depths, my feet sank deeper into their holes. A large wave pounded into my knees and thighs, and as the ocean sucked its tendrils back into its enormous mass, the sand reached up to my ankles and held me firmly in place.

The ocean shoreline teaches us a valuable lesson about standing still and sinking at the same time. Though standing motionless, we still manage to sink deeper into the sand. Why? Because although we are not moving, the water and sand around us are constantly in motion. It reminds me of our relationship with God. If we're not intentionally moving toward Him, we are, in effect, moving farther away. How is that possible? Because God is always on the move, always working, and always pursuing. If we're not moving with Him, we'll get left behind. In the same way, if we're not living like Jesus, we're living against Him. It's just like standing on the ocean's shore: if we're standing still, we're sinking.

God knew this truth about us, and it's one more reason why He sent His son Jesus to us. We know the Christmas story, right? God sent His only son, Jesus, to be born as a baby on earth. Mary, a virgin, would be his mother, and Joseph would be his father. An angel appeared to Joseph to explain these things.

> As he considered this, an angel of the Lord appeared to him in a dream. "Joseph, son of David," the angel said, "do not be afraid to take Mary as your wife. For the child within her was conceived by the Holy Spirit. And she will have a son, and you are to name him Jesus, for he will save his people from their sins."
>
> All of this occurred to fulfill the Lord's message through his prophet:
>
> "Look! The virgin will conceive a child! She will give birth to a son, and they will call him Immanuel, which means 'God is with us.'"
>
> (Matthew 1:20–23)

God came down to earth to dwell with us, thus the name "Immanuel." He arrived as an infant, meaning He was completely dependent on others for His survival and well-being. Jesus subjected Himself to the same needs we have for physical, emotional, and intellectual growth.

Have we ever stopped to consider why God chose to leave behind heaven for a limited lifetime on earth? Why did He choose to arrive in complete human and infant frailty, rather than power? Why did He choose to arrive in poverty and obscurity, rather than fame and fanfare? Why did He choose suffering over security?

God wanted to get as close to us as possible, and that meant subjecting Himself to our common, shared, human experiences. Furthermore, He knew we would fail in our attempts to continually seek Him, so He sought us instead.

> *God wanted to get as close to us as possible, and that meant subjecting Himself to our common, shared, human experiences.*

Who were some of the first people on earth who did seek out Jesus? Besides His parents, who first recognized Him as the promised Jewish king and Messiah? It was the magi, or wise men, from lands to the east of Judea. These men were likely astrologers, scientists, mathematicians, and nomads of sorts. They were not Jewish in faith or heritage; therefore, they were outsiders.

> Jesus was born in Bethlehem in Judea, during the reign of King Herod. About that time some wise men from eastern lands arrived in Jerusalem, asking, "Where is the newborn king of the Jews? We saw his star as it rose, and we have come to worship him." . . .
>
> When they saw the star, they were filled with joy! They entered the house and saw the child with his mother, Mary, and they bowed down and worshiped him. Then they opened their treasure chests and gave him gifts of gold, frankincense, and myrrh.
>
> (Matthew 2:1–2, 10–11)

As a helpless baby, Jesus was laid in a feed trough for animals, yet even before He could speak, He drew people to Him. God never intended that magnetism to affect only the chosen Jewish people. Jesus drew near to all of humanity. God placed the bright star in the sky, marking the Savior's birthplace, for all people to see. Do our stars shine as brightly? Do we proffer Jesus in a way that attracts people of all faiths, races, and backgrounds to come and kneel before the Lord? Do we invite *all* people to draw near to Jesus, or only those we consider worthy of entering our sanctuaries?

> *Do we invite all people to draw near to Jesus, or only those we consider worthy of entering our sanctuaries?*

Jesus did not discriminate when it came to drawing near. Scripture tells us of countless times when Jesus specifically drew near to people who were suffering. We see this when He traveled to see Mary and Martha, Lazarus's sisters, after Lazarus's death. We see this when Jesus turned and approached the woman with the issue of bleeding who touched the hem of His garment. We see this numerous times when Jesus healed the sick and the demon-tormented.

Jesus instructed us to imitate His behavior and not turn from those in need.

> "Heal the sick, raise the dead, cure those with leprosy, and cast out demons. Give as freely as you have received!"
>
> (Matthew 10:8)

Do we draw near to those who are hurting, or do we turn away because it's more than we want to handle? Jesus shows us the healing power found in simply drawing near, listening, and recognizing another's suffering.

One of my mother's friends—who was also my youth group sponsor at the time—taught me this lesson. At fifteen years old, I'd lost my mother to cancer. One Sunday morning during worship, this friend, Macky, saw me crying. She moved over to where I was sitting, put her arm around me, and whispered in my ear, "Nicki, I wish I could take your pain away." Her words touched me like a salve on an open wound. I responded, or rather the Holy Spirit within me responded, "It's okay, Macky. You don't have to. Jesus already has." Macky didn't turn away from my grief-filled sobs, but instead, she drew near, and it eased my suffering.

Our collective human suffering provides one of the main reasons God chose to draw near to us by coming down to earth. Adam and Eve broke our relationship with our Creator, and until it is restored, we live in constant torment, much like I felt after my mother died. God sent Jesus as the solution to that problem. As Pastor David Payne says, "He chose to become one of us, so we could be one with Him." Because of our human frailty and sin, we couldn't get to God on our own, so God came down to us in the human form of Jesus.

Pastor and author Tim Keller said, "The founders of every major religion said, 'I'll show you how to find God.' Jesus said, 'I am God who has come to find you.'"[4]

How do we respond to our Savior drawing near in this way? We must walk a path of surrender. Jesus gave us everything He had to offer, and He expects no less from us in return. We must empty ourselves and recognize we are nothing without Him. God desires only the best for His beloved children, so He cannot tolerate divided loyalties. He knows anything the world gives us will be inferior to what He alone can offer.

Come close to God, and God will come close to you.
Wash your hands, you sinners; purify your hearts, for
your loyalty is divided between God and the world.

(James 4:8)

God loves us so much that He stopped waiting for us to come to Him, and He took the initiative to come to us. This miracle is not just confined to the first Christmas, though; God is always near and always drawing us closer. Just like the waves on the ocean's sand, He is constantly beckoning us to let go of the shore and dive deeper into our relationship with Him and those around us. Draw near to God and others, just like Jesus.

LIVE LIKE JESUS

Inside . . .

Do you tend to shy away or draw near to others when they are hurting? Imagine these scenarios: You're in the grocery store and see a stranger sobbing in the same aisle as you; you pull up to an intersection and see a person holding a sign asking for food or money right beside your driver's side window; a woman in your Bible study class has just been diagnosed with breast cancer. Try to identify why you respond the way you do.

. . . and Out

Intentionally reach out to someone in need. Draw near to this person and focus on simply listening and being physically present with him or her. Be the kind of friend you will want when your day of need arises.

Who's Afraid of the Dark?

—— Bring the light like Jesus ——

My son grew increasingly agitated, and I sensed the bedtime battle beginning. Like a showdown at the O.K. Corral, I sensed the sun going down and bystanders clearing our immediate area.

I felt completely exhausted from the prior events of the day: unpleasant surprises, tantrums, messes, mom-chauffeuring three kids all over town, supper duties, and homework help. Still, I mustered every last ounce of patience I could find.

"Where is he?" Johnathan whined.

"Where is who, Sweetie?" I asked.

"I can't go to bed without him!" he threatened, throwing the sheet and blanket around frantically.

"Look at me," I implored. "What are you talking about?"

He sighed with exasperation. "My yite boy!"

Trying to understand, I repeated to him, "Your yite boy?"

"Noooo, my *wite* boy," he explained.

"Oh! You mean your *white* boy?" I asked, finally getting somewhere. But then I realized I still had no clue what he meant by his "white boy."

I desperately shoved my head underneath the toddler-sized bed and discovered Buzz Lightyear there. I proudly held him up and asked, "Is this him? Your *light* boy?"

"Yes!!" Johnathan ecstatically exclaimed. "There's my yite boy!"

Just like a child clutching a toy at bedtime and begging for a nightlight, we instinctively know we are meant for light, not darkness. When we find ourselves in the dark, we cease to grow and thrive. Ironically, we know we can't have light without darkness, for the two must coexist.

At the beginning of the disciple John's testimony, he refers to Jesus as both the Word and the light.

> The Word gave life to everything that was created, and his life brought light to everyone. The light shines in the darkness, and the darkness can never extinguish it.
>
> (John 1:4–5)

The darkness can never overcome the light. Jesus has vanquished evil and triumphed over death. Jesus also proclaimed Himself the light of the world, in whom there is no darkness at all.

> Jesus spoke to the people once more and said, "I am the light of the world. If you follow me, you won't have to walk in darkness, because you will have the light that leads to life."
>
> (John 8:12)

Jesus recommends we turn away from sin and invites us to enjoy abundant life by following Him.

Consider this: Jesus came down from heaven to earth, giving up a great deal of His knowledge and supernatural power to become human, like us. He must have felt out of place here, being human as well as divine. How did Jesus handle this strange juxtaposition, of claiming Himself as the light of the world while also walking around in a world ruled by the enemy (John 12:31)? The answer is that Jesus brought a little heaven down to earth everywhere He went. In other words, Jesus brought light into every dark situation He encountered. And we can, too.

Biblically speaking, what is this "light"? I believe a good synonym might be "truth." Jesus is the truth in the same sense that God is the truth. Everything right, good, holy, and life-affirming comes from God. Jesus is God in human form, for the benefit of our understanding God better. Therefore, when Jesus's light, or truth, shines in our lives, we see ourselves and our circumstances through the lens of God's will and love for us. Clarity opens up before us. We see

> *The more we step into God's light, the more His light shines in and through us, drawing others to Him.*

things as God intends them to be, not just as they are. The more we step into God's light, the more His light shines in and through us, drawing others to Him.

Jesus provides us with a literal example of this philosophy and "eye-opening" when He healed a man born blind.

> As Jesus was walking along, he saw a man who had been blind from birth. "Rabbi," his disciples asked him, "why was this man born blind? Was it because of his own sins or his parents' sins?"

> "It was not because of his sins or his parents' sins," Jesus answered. "This happened so the power of God could be seen in him. We must quickly carry out the tasks assigned us by the one who sent us. The night is coming, and then no one can work. But while I am here in the

world, I am the light of the world."

(John 9:1–5)

Jesus explains the blind man's affliction was not due to any sin on his or even his parents' behalf. He says the man suffers from blindness so He can heal him and display the power of God. Jesus goes on to explain that a time approaches when He, the light, will no longer be on the earth, and these types of healing may not be possible.

This particular healing enraged the Pharisees because Jesus accomplished it on a Sabbath day. The formerly blind man was called before a group of Pharisees to give his account. The Pharisees, having listened to the man tell his story of healing multiple times, refused to believe him.

> "Look!" the man exclaimed. "I told you once. Didn't you listen? Why do you want to hear it again? Do you want to become his disciples, too?"
>
> Then they cursed him and said, "You are his disciple, but we are disciples of Moses! We know God spoke to Moses, but we don't even know where this man comes from."
>
> "Why, that's very strange!" the man replied. "He healed my eyes, and yet you don't know where he comes from? We know that God doesn't listen to sinners, but he is ready to hear those who worship him and do his will. Ever since the world began, no one has been able to open the eyes of someone born blind. If this man were not from God, he couldn't have done it."
>
> (John 9:27–33)

The formerly blind man nailed the heart of the message when he claimed no person in all of history had been capable of bringing sight to the blind—of bringing light into someone's eyes that had previously known only darkness. He emphasized that only a man sent from God could do such a miraculous thing. Jesus was that healer . . . and that light.

> This is the message we heard from Jesus and now declare to you: God is light, and there is no darkness in him at all. So we are lying if we say we have fellowship with God but go on living in spiritual darkness; we are not practicing the truth. But if we are living in the light, as God is in the light, then we have fellowship with each other, and the blood of Jesus, his Son, cleanses us from all sin.
>
> (1 John 1:5–7)

We can live like Jesus and bring light into others' lives by receiving His atonement for our sins and by seeking relationship and fellowship with God and others. We don't need special toys or night lights to make us feel safe and loved. No wickedness or evil exists in our Savior, and by clinging to Him, we can live a life focused on eternity and truth and not on this dark world. Just like Jesus, we can then share that light with everyone around us.

Live like Jesus

Inside . . .

Ask Jesus to shine His light into the corners of your heart and the hidden aspects of your life. Allow His truth and light to penetrate all the places where darkness may reside in you.

. . . and Out

We cannot share the light—God's truth—if we don't know it ourselves. Spend time reading the Bible and studying Scripture. Ask God to alert you to situations you may encounter where you can act as a light-bearer for Him.

Don't Cry Over Spilled . . . Coffee

—— *Think like Jesus, part 1* ——

M y head was pounding and snot was dripping. I was convulsively coughing, relentlessly sneezing, and running late. After shivering under blankets all morning and into the afternoon, I'd barely pulled myself together to make the short drive to pick up my youngest child from elementary school. Dirty hair shoved under a ballcap and no makeup on, I donned a mask to protect others from the bronchitis that had taken up residence in my body. In the ultimate of ironies, my sick self needed to take my healthy child to the pediatrician for a routine checkup and medication authorization. We arrived at the doctor's office only to find out the appointment was canceled and had previously been rescheduled, but I had forgotten to delete today's original appointment in my calendar app. Then, I learned the doctor was not even in the office, so I couldn't get the authorization for the refill request my child needed for his medication, meaning I would have to make this same trip back to the doctor's office the next day just to pick up the slip of paper with the prescription on it.

So, we left the doctor's office and stopped at the grocery store on the way home because I needed to find something easy to make for supper because, despite being sick, all these humans who lived in my house still expected me to feed them. Go figure. I also needed some hot tea and throat lozenges due to the bronchitis, and because after a breast cancer scare last week, the doctor said I have cysts and need to watch my caffeine intake. I claimed insult to injury on that one.

We arrived home and I opened my child's homework folder to find that his teacher moved his behavior clip not once, but twice, because *last week* I forgot to sign the folder two days in a row. Was this due to my preoccupation with a cancer scare? Likely. Apparently, my child is being punished this week for my failures last week. So, when I abandoned the decaf tea and allowed myself a blissful cup of hot, steaming coffee to help me remain upright through the remainder of the afternoon, and then said cup went flying across the kitchen counter—spilling its contents all over the floor, cabinet, counter, and walls—and my favorite mug shattered into a thousand shards all over the tile floor where I stood barefoot, I decided it was okay to cry over spilled . . . coffee.

We've all been here, in this place where everything goes wrong at the same time. If you are anything like me, your mind starts reciting a litany of complaints like the long narrative above. That is exactly how my mind works during times like these: in overdrive, one thought furiously following the next with no breaks from the circular track on which it rides. Note that nowhere in my tirade did I communicate the little blessings of the day: the sweet hug from my son when he climbed into the car after school, or the young cashier at the grocery store who kindly asked if she could ask someone to find the herbal tea I couldn't locate myself, or my ability to stay home and rest in a warm, comfortable, safe house when I was ill. All these things happened today, too, but I chose to focus on the negative.

Getting caught in a cycle of negativity often feels effortless. We think if we recite a long list of grievances, we'll experience some kind of catharsis at its conclusion. We think if we recount the many unfair things that happened to us recently, that the sympathy we may receive from others will act like a balm to our spirit. We think if we moan and groan and stomp our feet like the spiritual toddlers we are, we'll get all our yucky feelings out into the open and suddenly feel better.

Think again, because none of these things work. If anything, our complaining, mumbling, and grumbling coil us up even tighter. Now we are spitting fire and anger as well as self-pity, all because we experienced a rather ordinary day in an extraordinarily fallen world.

Greek philosopher Epictetus said, "It's not what happens to you, but how you react to it that matters."[5] We hear similar refrains from life coaches and motivational speakers from all over the world. But what does this look like in real life? How do we learn to react *better*? How do we stop spinning out and instead keep our wits— and our faith—tightly about us? The answer lies in the battleground of our minds. Where our minds go, our hearts, mouths, and bodies will follow.

> Don't copy the behavior and customs of this world, but let God transform you into a new person by changing the way you think. Then you will learn to know God's will for you, which is good and pleasing and perfect.
>
> (Romans 12:2)

As difficult as it is to imagine, God can change the way we think. Let's look at this verse in stages.

First, Paul tells us in this verse we need to stop. Full stop. Stop acting like everybody else. Stop calling a friend and launching into a tirade about what Ms. Snooty So-and-So said in the carpool line today. Stop racing onto social media and firing off angry posts about all the trivial things wrong in the world today. Stop taking pleasure in venting about minor inconveniences when real suffering and horrible injustice exist all around us—in our neighborhoods, churches, communities, and world. Just stop.

Second, we need to let God change the way we think. Now, this one isn't easy. This will take time. Dive into the Word of God. Study the life of Jesus. Take care to note when, how, and why He spoke, as these instances give us insight into His thoughts and mind. Be intentional about prayer time and study, because God will reveal more and more of Himself to us during those times. As we seek Him earnestly and yield more of ourselves to His authority, we allow the Holy Spirit greater access to our minds and spirits, and then God can begin His transformative work within us.

Where our minds go, our hearts, mouths, and bodies will follow.

Third, this thought-transformation process is accompanied by the process of sanctification. Now, sanctification is a big religious word referring to the process of becoming pure and holy like God. Sanctification is never finished on this side of heaven. However, we can choose to deepen our relationship with God and become more like Jesus. This allows God to cleanse us and the Holy Spirit to prompt us to know how to act more in line with His will.

Knowing the mind of Jesus will help us change our own minds and thought processes. We can read the Bible a thousand times, but if we don't allow the Holy Spirit the opportunity to transform our minds and our ways of thinking, we will simply impose *our own* ideas and biases into the Scripture we read. If we want to think like Jesus, we first must get to know Him, and then we must seek the transformation and sanctification only He can offer.

We must first stop conforming to this world's thought patterns and resulting behaviors. Then, we can draw nearer to God in prayer and study, allowing the Holy Spirit to transform and sanctify us. When we do, we will begin to see the world through a different lens, just as Jesus sees. Then, even on trying days when we need to cry over spilled coffee, we can think more about God's blessings than the world's challenges.

LIVE LIKE JESUS

Inside . . .

Do you have any thought patterns you now recognize as running counter to the "mind of Christ?" Don't be afraid to call them out.

. . . and Out

Allow God to change the way you think. Ask for the Holy Spirit's help. Commit to spending time in prayer and study, and submit yourself to God's processes of transformation and sanctification.

The One When God's Hands Got Wet

—— Think like Jesus, part 2 ——

My son grew visibly excited one day as we drove over the big bridge in town that crosses the Guadalupe River. The bouncing preschooler's sudden animation surprised me since we cross that same bridge daily.

"Mommy!" he exclaimed. "I see the river!"

"Mm-hmm," I replied. "I see it too, Sweetie."

My son got very still, quiet, and pensive in his car seat. "His hands are wet!" he suddenly said.

"What?" I questioned. "Whose hands are wet?"

"God's," Johnathan replied in his tiny voice, "from Him making the river."

I nearly drove off the road, y'all. These moments—the tiny glimpses into how my son's mind works—just astound me.

> *Whatever we choose to focus on, we begin to see everywhere.*

I think we can divide people into two basic categories, based on differences in how our minds process our experiences and how we view the world around us. One group sees the world and most of what it holds as bad or in need of correction, and the other group sees the world and most of what it holds as good and more right than wrong. Why is this? I believe it's because our personal experiences shape our perceptions of the world around us. This results in a simple truth: whatever we choose to focus on, we begin to see everywhere.

How often do we read and interpret Scripture through the lens of our hurt, prejudice, shame, and insecurities? Do we try to understand the cultural norms of the geographic area and period in which a scriptural passage was written, or do we only try to apply it to our current circumstances? Do we twist our image of Jesus to fit how we think He should look and act, or do we take Him exactly as He is?

> "My thoughts are nothing like your thoughts," says the LORD. "And my ways are far beyond anything you could imagine. For just as the heavens are higher than the earth, so my ways are higher than your ways and my thoughts higher than your thoughts."
>
> (Isaiah 55:8–9)

We are called to think like Jesus—not to know everything like only He can, but instead to follow His thought patterns. So, what did Jesus choose to spend His time thinking about? Where was His focus?

For one, Jesus focused on the unseen, not just the tangible things around Him.

> When I was a child, I spoke and thought and reasoned as a child. But when I grew up, I put away childish things. Now we see things imperfectly, like puzzling reflections in a mirror, but then we will see everything with perfect clarity. All that I know now is partial and incomplete, but

then I will know everything completely, just as God now knows me completely.

(1 Corinthians 13:11–12)

I have a large, rain glass window in my bathroom. I can see light, shadows, and large shapes through it, but not distinct objects. One day I watched a shadowy figure move across the yard close to this window. Something was out there, and it was alive and moving. I didn't know if it was an animal or a person, but it was close to the other side of that glass. I couldn't see it clearly, but that didn't mean it wasn't out there, moving near me.

The same is true of the Holy Spirit and the spirits in the heavenly realm. We know they are out there, all around us in a dimension we cannot clearly see. Jesus, having resided in heaven before coming to earth, knew this personally. Spiritual warfare is real, and He experienced it first-hand. I believe this colored His interpretation of earthly events. Jesus knew all too well how the story would play out: He would give His life in exchange for eternal victory over evil. Jesus's thoughts had to be on the big picture, and on how every event and moment He experienced on earth would affect the end game of the world's salvation.

> In your relationships with one another, have the same mindset as Christ Jesus: Who, being in very nature God, did not consider equality with God something to be used to his own advantage; rather, he made himself nothing by taking the very nature of a servant, being made in human likeness. And being found in appearance as a man, he humbled himself by becoming obedient to death—even death on a cross!
>
> (Philippians 2:5–8 NIV)

When Jesus entered this world, He entered it with the eyes of an innocent baby. Unlike most of humankind, as Jesus grew up, He continued to view the world with an abundance of empathy and compassion. He extended an open invitation to salvation for all people, right in the middle of their mess and sin. He offered them love and acceptance first, then salvation and transformation second.

Jesus's focus wasn't on the world, but on loving the people of the world.

Is this how *we* think of the people around us? Valuable, worthy, and redeemable? I know I witness the opposite of this in conversations and on social media daily. For example, "those people" deserve their mess because they caused it, or "those people" don't deserve safety, food security, and a warm roof over their heads, because they haven't "earned" it.

Friends, these are not the thoughts of Christ! Jesus wasn't first to criticize or blame . . . He was first to come alongside, reach down, and lift up. If we choose to focus on our differences, how can we possibly see the many ways we are alike? Compassion and empathy suffer in the wake of self-righteous people. "Me and mine first" never came out of the mouth of our Savior.

> Since you have been raised to new life with Christ, set your sights on the realities of heaven, where Christ sits in the place of honor at God's right hand. Think about the things of heaven, not the things of earth.
>
> (Colossians 3:1–2)

Jesus thought differently than the world around Him because His focus was on God, not on the world. Christ knew the Father intimately and focused on God's character, purpose, and motivation to love us and draw us into a relationship with Him. Jesus's focus wasn't on the world, but on loving the people of the world.

> And now, dear brothers and sisters, one final thing. Fix your thoughts on what is true, and honorable, and right, and pure, and lovely, and admirable. Think about things that are excellent and worthy of praise.
>
> (Philippians 4:8)

I sometimes use this verse from Philippians as a litmus test for my thoughts. Is it true? Is it honorable? Is it right, pure, lovely, or admirable? Is it excellent and worthy of praise? If not, then maybe I shouldn't be focusing my mind on it. At best, I should take those thoughts to God in prayer and seek His truth and perspective on them. I know I could spare myself a great deal of agony and emotional and relational turmoil if I could learn to use this thought test more consistently.

Friends, we are called to think like Jesus. That means setting our minds on things above and focusing on the character and plans of the Heavenly Father. My son saw the same river he's seen almost every day of his life, but one particular day he chose to focus on the God who made it and on His experience in creating it. God's hands got wet, y'all. For Johnathan, that changed everything. Let's choose—or rather, let's *make up our minds*—to focus on Jesus and adopt the mind of Christ. When we do, everything will change and look different to us, too.

Live like Jesus

Inside . . .

Where is your focus? What do you think about the most? Compare this to what Jesus spent His time thinking about.

. . . and Out

Strive to recognize critical and/or self-serving thoughts the instant they pop into your mind. Make a habit of saying an immediate prayer asking God to redirect your thoughts towards Him. As often as you can, focus your thoughts on Jesus and allow the Holy Spirit to guide you from thought into action.

The Terrible, Horrible, No Good, Very Bad Thanksgiving

—— Find Contentment like Jesus ——

The Carlson Thanksgiving was—for all intents and purposes—canceled. The morning after the school break began, we discovered my sister and her family could not come for the holiday due to COVID-19 exposure. Within two hours, we found out one of our nuclear family members had also been exposed to COVID. Later that day, my mother-in-law called saying she had been exposed. Out of three different households, we encountered three different origins of exposure. It was my first time hosting Thanksgiving, and it was over before it even began. I felt like I'd taken a sucker punch to the gut.

I then found out my oldest daughter, in her sophomore year in college, could not come home for the break. She was starting finals that week and couldn't take the risk of getting sick and not being able to complete the semester. One evening that week, she parked on the other side of the white fence bordering our front yard and waved to us from a distance. We visited briefly that night and then she left to spend the holiday with another family. I hadn't seen her in many weeks, and I couldn't even hug her. It broke my maternal heart, but I smiled as best I could while I waved goodbye after our all-too-short visit from an all-too-safe distance.

On Thanksgiving Day, our little foursome (instead of the twenty-something we had planned) sat around the breakfast table (instead of the newly decorated dining room table) and ate takeout from a local restaurant (instead of a homemade feast lovingly prepared by many hands). As my husband prayed his heartfelt thanks to the God who has blessed us abundantly, tears ran down my cheeks. All I could hear was my silent prayer:

"God, forgive me for wanting more than what You have deemed fit to give. Forgive me for craving anything that doesn't come from You. Help me to know this is enough, God. Help me to stop wanting more."

That prayer became a meditation for me over the next few days, as the four of us all worked hard to navigate disappointment and sadness, as well as joy and thanksgiving. We gave each other grace, space, and lots of hugs. Slowly, I felt my heart begin to change.

I realized I often struggle to trust in God's abundance, but I also struggle to trust in His withholding. I realized both stem from a lack of faith and result in my discontent. True contentment requires detachment from our outward circumstances and a reliance on God's resources alone.

> *True contentment requires detachment from our outward circumstances and a reliance on God's resources alone.*

Paul taught this same lesson in the letter he wrote to the Philippians while he was in prison.

> Not that I was ever in need, for I have learned how to be content with whatever I have. I know how to live on almost nothing or with everything. I have learned the

secret of living in every situation, whether it is with a full stomach or empty, with plenty or little. For I can do everything through Christ, who gives me strength.

(Philippians 4:11–13)

Paul described how his circumstances did not dictate his level of contentment, and by relying on the supernatural provision of Christ he could accomplish things beyond his human weaknesses.

One of my signature weak points is anxiety—that catch-all word for feeling "ill content." Middle ground, periods of waiting, and promises not yet fulfilled often cause me to stumble, and the enemy knows it. Some of the worst anxiety I've ever faced was waiting for my first book to be edited, typeset, and then released. My mind became fertile ground for all kinds of negative, outlandish thoughts and fears. Were my actual circumstances terrible? Absolutely not. Were my circumstances what I wanted right at that moment? Again, they were not. I wasn't trusting in God's plan, timing, and provision.

Now, during similar circumstances, I stop and force myself to identify five things I am grateful for in that moment, and then I thank God for those blessings. Turning my thoughts back to God and His faithfulness and power saves me from myself every time.

Don't worry about anything; instead, pray about everything. Tell God what you need, and thank him for all he has done. Then you will experience God's peace, which exceeds anything we can understand. His peace will guard your hearts and minds as you live in Christ Jesus.

(Philippians 4:6–7)

Another way I practice gratitude and contentment is by meditating on God's promises in His Word. I remind myself He loves me

(1 John 4:16), His plans are for my good (Jer. 29:11), His timing is perfect (1 Pet. 3:9), and He has remained faithful in the past (1 Thess. 5:23–25). I utilize Scripture—the ultimate weapon—in battles the enemy wages in my mind.

Where our minds go, our moods usually follow. Contentment tends to ebb and flow with our emotions, which ultimately betray us and are easily manipulated. We can positively alter our moods, though. We can listen to Christian or upbeat music, meditate, take a nature walk, talk to a spiritual mentor or friend, read Scripture, or journal. And of course, we can tap into the deep abiding well of joy that never runs dry: Jesus. Our Savior is never moody. We never need to worry that Jesus will be too irritable, busy, or frazzled to listen to our prayers.

> *If I find myself wanting more than God has chosen to give me, I'm not trusting that He is acting in my best interest.*

Jesus instructs us, saying:

> "So don't worry about these things, saying, 'What will we eat? What will we drink? What will we wear?' These things dominate the thoughts of unbelievers, but your heavenly father already knows all your needs. Seek the Kingdom of God above all else, and live righteously, and he will give you everything you need."
>
> (Matthew 6:31–33)

If I find myself wanting more than God has chosen to give me, I'm not trusting that He is acting in my best interest. According to Jesus, God knows all my needs. So, if I want my circumstances to line up with my dreams instead of His plans, I want my way more than I want His future for me. This sort of wanting "more" represents a lack of faith. It's thinking my way is better than His way. These are guaranteed ways to never find contentment.

The truth is, comparison of any kind will steal our satisfaction. We can always find people with more—more things, more ease, more attractiveness, more fitness. Only after we stop making these kinds of comparisons can we emerge as the best versions of ourselves. Because none of us earned a single blessing we hold, we should focus on the good gifts we've been given and show gratitude to God for His grace in offering them.

We now know the keys to our discontent, so what is the key to our contentment? Jesus shows us the way.

> "I have loved you even as the Father has loved me. Remain in my love. When you obey my commandments, you remain in my love, just as I obey my Father's commandments and remain in his love. I have told you these things so that you will be filled with my joy. Yes, your joy will overflow! This is my commandment: Love each other in the same way I have loved you."
>
> (John 15:9–12)

Jesus instructs us to remain, or abide, in His perfect love; furthermore, we are to obey His commandments and—specifically—love others with the same love He holds for us. The key to our contentment is fully and completely resting in the perfect, all-consuming love of our Heavenly Father, and in response to that love, sharing it with others. Our contentment resides in God's love for us and in the knowledge that He walks beside us, willing and preparing goodness in our lives.

There's no time like the present to seek Godly contentment, because the present is a gift we should not leave unopened . . . even if it is a takeout container of a subpar Thanksgiving dinner.

LIVE LIKE JESUS

Inside . . .

Do you find it natural to remain content, or do you find it easier to become annoyed, aggravated, and disgruntled by others and the world around you? Is the thief of comparison stealing your contentment?

. . . and Out

Name one area of yourself or your life that you compare to others. Does this lead to greater or less contentment? Describe how focusing on God's love for you might increase your feeling of fulfillment. Now, name one practice that will lead to greater contentment with your life and your Savior.

Watch Out for Falling Exercise Bikes and Other Answered Prayers

—— Trust like Jesus ——

"You need to find a stationary exercise bike," the physical therapist told me. He was treating me for debilitating migraines and herniated discs in my neck, the not-so-lovely parting gifts of a speeding driver who had veered into our lane and rammed us into a dividing wall on the interstate. Our car was totaled.

I didn't want to spend a ton of money on brand-new exercise equipment because my condition was temporary and because we also needed to buy a new vehicle, so I set off on a search for what I needed. I scoured social media sites, online garage sales, yard sales, estate sales, local gyms . . . everywhere I could look.

Now, I measure all of 5-foot-nothing, which means most exercise bikes, despite their adjustment features, do not fit my body the way these machines are designed to fit people. They're made for adults, and apparently "5-foot-nothing" means I am closer to the size of a large child than a full-grown adult. If I'm stretching and straining to reach the pedals, I risk greater injury to my already injured back and neck. In this particular case, I needed one of those stationary bikes that sits low to the ground where your legs stretch out forward and your feet pedal out in front of you, rather than sitting tall and upright above the pedals in a traditional diamond frame and pedaling downward.

I exhausted every means I could think of to locate what I needed. I started to lose hope, but as a last-ditch effort, I decided to pray about it. "God, please help me find an affordable stationary bike I can use that will fit my body the way it's supposed to. Amen."

Now, did I actually trust God was going to just deliver—by some gym equipment fairy—an exercise bike to my doorstep? Did I expect one to just fall from the sky? No, I did not. I did, however, expect God to offer some kind of help.

Well, He definitely helped. He didn't quite deliver an exercise bike to my front door, but He did deliver one directly across the street. The next day after praying, I looked outside and saw a stationary bike sitting on the curb of my across-the-street neighbor's house. I walked across the street to ask about it, and my neighbors said they left it on the curb for bulk trash pick-up that day. Of course, it fit me perfectly! A mere $7 in parts later, and I was spinning for all the neighborhood to see.

This experience taught me a great deal about trusting God. We don't have to understand His "means" to have faith in His outcome. We don't have to assume God will require a lot of sweat equity on our part, because sometimes He just makes the answer easy and obvious for us. We don't have to claim perfect faith when we ask God for help because His goal is building an intimate, trusting relationship with us more than anything else.

Jesus perfectly modeled for us how to trust God. Probably the most obvious example of this occurs near the end of His life, in the garden of Gethsemane. We know Jesus struggled with knowing of His impending arrest and crucifixion, so He poured His heart out to His Father in prayer.

> He went on a little farther and bowed with his face to
> the ground, praying, "My Father! If it is possible, let this
> cup of suffering be taken away from me. Yet I want your
> will to be done, not mine."
>
> (Matthew 26:39)

Jesus expressed His ultimate trust in His Father's love and faithfulness when He surrendered to God's will for His life, rather than insisting on His own will. This signaled not only His trust in God's ultimate plan but also His trust that God would sustain and strengthen Him through impending difficult times. He trusted God to abide with Him and remain faithful to Him. He trusted in the perfection of God's timing of the events transpiring in His life. Jesus trusted God to fulfill His promises and bring goodness into the world.

> And we know that God causes everything to work
> together for the good of those who love God and are
> called according to his purpose for them.
>
> (Romans 8:28)

In these moments in the garden, Jesus put His faith in the God of His past who was His faithful provider, in the God of His present who was His comforter and strength, and in the God of His future who would be victorious and true to His word. Author and Pastor Tony Evans says, "We often doubt what God will do because we have forgotten what God has done."[6] Jesus didn't fall victim to this forgetfulness. We should remember that the God of Jesus's past, present, and future is the same God of our lifetimes. He was and is and is to come. We can trust in this.

In addition to seeing how Jesus demonstrated trust in God during His own life, we also find examples from Scripture of how He nurtured other people's trust in God. In the Gospel of Mark, we see Jesus draw near to a father desperate for his son's healing from demonic possession. The father struggles between wanting to believe in the healing power of Christ, and truly trusting in His ability to perform such a miracle. The disciples tried to bring the demon out of the boy unsuccessfully before Jesus arrived on the scene.

> So they brought the boy. But when the evil spirit saw Jesus, it threw the child into a violent convulsion, and he fell to the ground, writhing and foaming at the mouth.
>
> "How long has this been happening?" Jesus asked the boy's father.
>
> He replied, "Since he was a little boy. The spirit often throws him into the fire or into water, trying to kill him. Have mercy on us and help us, if you can."
>
> "What do you mean, 'If I can'?" Jesus asked. "Anything is possible if a person believes."
>
> The father instantly cried out, "I do believe, but help me overcome my unbelief!"
>
> (Mark 9:20–24)

I love the honesty of this boy's father. Not wanting to lie to Jesus, he claims belief while also leaving room for his doubts. How does Jesus respond? He heals the boy and casts out the demon. Perfect faith was not what Jesus sought, but rather reliance on Him. Jesus did not chastise the father again for his lack of faith, but instead entered into the man's plight and pain and, despite his doubts, granted healing anyway. This father shows us it's possible to trust God without having all the answers. Christ wanted this father to feel seen, so He extended empathy, mercy, and grace to him, despite his questions.

How do we respond when others are questioning their faith in God? Do we draw near like Jesus did, or do we pull away? Do we offer a safe place for others' questions or do we shame them for their lack of belief or trust in God? How about when we are the ones questioning?

Jesus draws near and stands in the gap between our hearts and our heads . . . between our trust and our lack of trust.

When Jesus sees us wavering, He doesn't leave us to our demise. Like a parent running toward a newly-walking toddler who has fallen, God draws close, reaches down, picks us up, and puts us back on our feet again. He comes to us right where we are, questions and all because that's what love does. Jesus draws near and stands in the gap between our hearts and our heads . . . between our trust and our lack of trust.

> Those who know your name trust in you, for you, O LORD, do not abandon those who search for you.
>
> (Psalm 9:10)

We shouldn't need an exercise bike to fall out of the sky and land on us to know God has provided for us and is therefore worthy of our trust; but, sometimes, it helps. It also helps to remember the God that Jesus trusted in the garden is the same God we serve today, and He is the same God who raised Jesus from the dead just as

He said He would. He has proven Himself faithful time and again. Faithfulness is His very nature. In Him, we can trust.

Live like Jesus

Inside...

In what area of your life do you find it most difficult to trust God? In which corners of your life and mind do you struggle with doubts the most?

... and Out

Visualize some possible, positive outcomes that might occur if you trust God with these aspects of your life. Commit to praying about them. Read Scripture that reminds you of His promises to remain faithful to you, and post them in places you will see often. Ask God to help you surrender these matters entirely to Him. Remember: God is worthy of your trust.

Give Me a Break!

—— *Rest like Jesus* ——

Years ago, my pint-sized terror came racing into the room and whispered urgently, "Mom! Shhhhhh!"

I whispered dramatically in response, "What is going on? It's still rest time, Sweetie."

He answered, "We have to be very quiet! There's a fake man sleeping in my room!"

I instantly realized three things following his impromptu announcement. First, my little man's insistence on making others bend to his will knew absolutely no bounds, even during imaginary play. His motto was firmly, "What I am doing—and what I want—matters. Join me. Or else." Second, he did understand the need to be quiet when someone was sleeping, despite Saturday and Sunday morning scream-fests which provided evidence to the contrary. And third, he apparently understood the importance of naps; which, by the way, he was supposed to be taking at that very moment.

This child often left me astonished and speechless. Trying to get him to take a nap was like asking a wild hyena to come to a formal tea party. He was a great deal kinder and nicer after some rest, though. Aren't we all?

This year, I found myself tired and in need of rest like never before. In the last year, my second child graduated from high school while her sister and I watched via television from the couch, unable to attend because we had COVID-19. Big sister fainted, twice, the morning of little sister's graduation, and at that point, we realized our sinus infections weren't just sinus infections. We canceled the family reunion/graduation party for that weekend. We rescheduled the senior trip. Two weeks later, we embarked on a short, family vacation (while continuing to recover from COVID) and tried to celebrate the end of the school year together.

While on vacation, one of my special "other" mothers passed away from cancer. Heartbroken, we left our vacation early and drove more than twelve hours straight so I could make it to the funeral. A few short weeks later, my mother-in-law died tragically and suddenly. We grieved while trying to prepare my second oldest to leave home for the first time and head off to college. Within weeks, our first family pet died, just a short few weeks after being diagnosed with liver cancer—ironically, the same cancer that killed my mother when I was fifteen years old. One child received the news she needed two invasive, long-recovery foot surgeries over the next two years, and that same child scheduled wisdom teeth removal for Christmas break. When Christmas break arrived, we endured a heart-wrenching period of teen rebellion and our adopted son firmly pushing us away, followed by the realization he located and reached out to his birth family without sharing the process with us. Suffice it to say, this wasn't the easiest period in my motherhood journey.

So, what did we decide to do amid all this chaos? We bought a new office building for my husband and moved his law practice. Also, we built a house next door for my dad and stepmother and helped them move as well.

A college senior, a college freshman, a freshman in high school, and everyone struggling with extreme loss, grief, change, and stress. I give it zero stars: Would not recommend.

So yes, "tired and in need of rest" was an understatement. My husband and I managed to get away for a week that summer (only after canceling our original vacation plans due to hurricanes and re-planning an entire trip one week before leaving), and I think I slept for over half of our time away. No joke—I was sleeping eleven to twelve hours at night and taking at least an hour-long nap every afternoon. I asked my husband how many nights in a row he thought a person could sleep that much, and he replied, "As long as they need to, Baby. Sweet dreams."

I relay all this information not to host a pity party for myself. On the contrary, I know nothing that happened in the past year is crazy abnormal, and I know God has blessed this life of mine way beyond what I deserve. I say all this to remind us that life is cyclical and increasingly cliché: it's full of mountains and valleys, light and darkness, highs and lows, activity and rest.

We often forget that the first book of the Bible—the creation story of the world itself—provides us with the first example of the need for rest.

> On the seventh day God had finished his work of creation, so he rested from all his work. And God blessed the seventh day and declared it holy, because it was the day when he rested from all his work of creation.
>
> (Genesis 2:2–3)

Our all-powerful God took a rest! Later, we see our divine God walking the earth in the human body of Jesus, and He also needed rest.

> The apostles returned to Jesus from their ministry tour
> and told him all they had done and taught. Then Jesus
> said, "Let's go off by ourselves to a quiet place and rest
> awhile." He said this because there were so many people
> coming and going that Jesus and his apostles didn't even
> have time to eat. So they left by boat for a quiet place,
> where they could be alone.
>
> (Mark 6:30–32)

I love this passage in Mark because I relate to it so well: *they
didn't even have time to eat.* We've all been there at times, when life
is so busy, crazy, and chaotic, and the demands on our time so great
that we can't even squeeze in a quick meal. It's unhealthy for a great
many reasons. But note how Jesus responded. He suggested they go
away somewhere quiet, just He and His closest friends, and rest. It's
a lesson we can and should take to heart.

Earlier in the book of Mark, we see Jesus making another request
for rest. After a long day of teaching and preaching to large crowds,
Jesus suggested He and His friends steal away to a quieter place.

> As evening came, Jesus said to his disciples, "Let's cross
> to the other side of the lake." So they took Jesus in
> the boat and started out, leaving the crowds behind
> (although other boats followed).
>
> (Mark 4:35–36)

What happened next? Our Savior promptly fell asleep! This is
the same boat trip during which a furious storm arose and the disciples feared they were perishing, and during which Jesus *slept*. He
knew He needed a break from the pressure of the crowds and from

the exhaustion of teaching. He knew He needed a respite before continuing to minister to others.

If the God of the Universe—in both divine and human form—needed to rest, then how much more do we?

Today, I give you permission to rest. For a few moments, put this book aside and close your eyes. Breathe deeply in and out. Relax your shoulders and your jaw. Ask God to show you the kind of rest you need, and then make a plan to act on it. Learning to take a break for ourselves may not happen overnight, and starting the process may even lead to unwholesome feelings of guilt. However, our contentment, health, and productivity will only increase with the practice of rest. Gradually, we will realize how much better we feel: stronger, more patient, more competent, and less overwhelmed. Most importantly, when we clear out the junk and noise in our heads and hearts, we can hear our Heavenly Father more clearly, draw near to Him, and energetically join Him in the work He has for us.

If the God of the Universe—in both divine and human form—needed to rest, then how much more do we?

And that's worth delving into a little quiet rest time . . . imaginary nap mates are optional.

LIVE LIKE JESUS

Inside...

Do you prioritize rest, or do you try to "push through" your body's signs when it signals its need for recovery? Why do you think God created our bodies with a distinct need for rest?

...and Out

Rest means more than just sleep. It can also mean time alone, time spent away from home and work, time with close friends and family, and time doing things that relax your mind and spirit. Find ways to incorporate different kinds of rest into your daily life, and note how your relationship with God deepens.

It's Time

—— Grieve like Jesus, part 1 ——

Picture a pregnant young mother, sweaty and contracting in pain, as the doctor announces to the room: "It's time." Time for what? Time for new life to enter this world. Now, picture the somber hospital room of an unresponsive elderly woman, her grown children surrounding her bedside, as the doctor announces to the room: "It's time." Time for what? Time for life to depart from this world.

I find it interesting how we mark arrivals and departures from this world with the same phrase: *It's time*. We react to these two experiences very differently, though. We generally respond to birth with joy and thanksgiving, and we usually respond to death with sadness and grief. In reality, birth is simply the spiritual being entering the physical world, and death is the physical body released as the spiritual being returns to the spiritual world. Both should be celebrated with thanksgiving, but as in all matters of life here on earth, we find it difficult to focus on the spiritual and ethereal while we are still stuck residing in the physical.

My friend Deana Blackburn often says she believes one of the most harmful teachings of contemporary Christianity is that God resides in heaven, which exists above us in the clouds. This causes a separation between God and us; furthermore, if we believe our loved ones reside in heaven, the separation from them is an unreach-able chasm as well . . . at least while we are still living. In truth, the Bible tells us God is always with us. Jesus's actual name, Emmanuel, means "God with us." Scripture tells us God is also present through His Holy Spirit.

> I can never escape from your Spirit! I can never get away from your presence! If I go up to heaven, you are there; if I go down to the grave, you are there.
>
> (Psalm 139:7–8)

The veil between the physical and spiritual realms is not as thick as we might think. Jesus illustrates this point by bringing back from the dead three different people in His lifetime: Lazarus (John 11), the daughter of Jairus (Luke 8), and the son of the widow in Nain (Luke 7).

As we know, Jesus personally straddled this line between spir-itual (deity) and physical (human). As such, He gives us insight into both experiences. We can see Jesus's double-faceted existence through the story of the death of His friend, Lazarus.

The eleventh chapter of John explains Jesus knew, even before He was told, that Lazarus had died. He also knew He would raise Lazarus from the dead. Both give credence to His deity.

> But when Jesus heard about it he said, "Lazarus's sick-ness will not end in death. No, it happened for the glory of God so that the Son of God will receive glory from this."
>
> (John 11:4)

Nevertheless, we read when Jesus encountered Lazarus's sister,

Mary, near Lazarus's tomb, Jesus—in His *humanity*—became quite emotional.

> When Mary arrived and saw Jesus, she fell at his feet and said, "Lord, if only you had been here, my brother would not have died."
>
> When Jesus saw her weeping and saw the other people wailing with her, a deep anger welled up within him, and he was deeply troubled.
>
> "Where have you put him?" he asked them.
>
> They told him, "Lord, come and see."
>
> Then Jesus wept.
>
> (John 11:32–35)

Why the outpouring of emotion from Jesus? Did He weep out of love for His friend, or out of compassion for His friend's sisters and family? Did Jesus cry because He realized He, too, would die in a matter of days, or did His tears come as a result of grief over our collective sin that continued to cause death and suffering in the world? Did He realize the act of raising Lazarus would be the final impetus for the religious leaders to come for His own life?

We don't know why Jesus wept, but verses 33 and 38 tell us He was also "angry" and "troubled." In His omniscience, Jesus not only knew firsthand what awaited Lazarus in the afterlife, but He also knew He was going to raise Lazarus from his deathbed. But knowing Lazarus's fate didn't make the difficult parts of his story any easier for Jesus to bear. The better question is not why Jesus reacted so passionately, but rather why we, as humans, think we can confront death in a less emotional way than Jesus did in His divinity.

Acknowledging emotional pain does not negate our faith, and acknowledging grief doesn't either. Jesus did not view His openly expressed emotions as evidence of a lack of faith or as doubts as to the goodness of the Heavenly Father. And what did He do next? He prayed, thanked God, spoke openly of His faith and trust in God, and thereby brought glory to the Father.

> *Acknowledging emotional pain does not negate our faith, and acknowledging grief doesn't either.*

Friends, we need to grieve like Jesus. We need to get angry, feel troubled, and weep. Stifling these emotions will not get us to a happier destination any faster. Like Jesus, we need to go to funerals or go visit the families of those who have lost loved ones, and we need to cry with them. We also need to willingly *accept* those visits from others if we are the ones suffering through loss. We need to pray, giving voice to thanksgiving, trust, and hope in God, just like Jesus did in the wake of Lazarus's death.

Some people say grief is the pain of loving and having to let go. That is why we gather together as we grieve, because holding on to each other makes it easier to let go of the person we've lost. We grieve with the hope of a reunion in heaven and never having to let go again. However, we fail to realize when death strips our false sense of security from us, we don't need to respond by fearing the future. We can instead embrace the new gift of truly embracing and appreciating the present, and no longer take the people and relationships in our lives for granted.

I think one of our biggest deficiencies in grief is constantly wondering, "How long will this take? How long do I have to feel this way?" Big emotions and vulnerability are difficult for us. We fail to recognize grief has no timetable, and the process never truly ends. Asking if grief includes a time limit is a sign of healing, though, because it means we can at least imagine feeling happiness and peace again. It helps greatly to acknowledge that our emotions and pain do not keep our loved ones' memories alive for us. These feelings do not keep us connected to them. Rather, everything those people deposited within us—their love, their lessons, our shared moments and memories—keeps us forever close. It's good to feel it all, but a time will come when it's okay to let the truly painful feelings recede. If God can create life from dust, rest assured He can create beauty and goodness from the remnants of our broken hearts.

Only a thin veil separates us from one another. In a truly strange and poignant way, nothing is sweeter than holding the hand of a loved one as he or she passes from this life into the eternal. The room becomes hushed and calm. The air feels different—charged almost, but in a completely tranquil way. God pulls the veil aside just long enough to welcome one of His children home. Overwhelming gratitude abounds for having shared life with this other person. It is a great honor to be present in a moment such as this . . . at the incredible instant when "It's time."

Live like Jesus

Inside . . .

Does knowing Jesus experienced grief offer you any comfort or encouragement when facing personal seasons of grief? Why or why not? Can you remember a time when you experienced the "thinness" of the veil between heaven and earth?

. . . and Out

Decide now to be the person who shows up for those who are grieving. Attend the service. Visit their loved ones. Send flowers, a meal, or even a simple handwritten note inside a card. Stay in touch. And don't forget to also accept such gifts when you are experiencing grief yourself.

It's *Not* Time

—— *Grieve like Jesus, part 2* ——

Wwe were never supposed to encounter death. Death entered our story only after Adam and Eve succumbed to the evil serpent's temptation in the garden of Eden. Until this point, humankind was free to eat from the Tree of Life and live forever. After they sinned, God banished Adam and Eve from the garden, meaning they could no longer eat from the Tree of Life, meaning they would eventually perish.

> The LORD God placed the man in the garden of Eden to tend and watch over it. But the LORD God warned him, "You may freely eat the fruit of every tree in the garden—except the tree of the knowledge of good and evil. If you eat its fruit, you are sure to die."
>
> (Genesis 2:15–17)

Does this mean death is a punishment? I don't believe so, even though at times it may feel that way. Death is a consequence. If death were a punishment, God would sentence us all to an eternity in these sick and sinful bodies we inhabit, rather than providing us an escape hatch to heaven (His name is Jesus) where we can enjoy complete intimacy and fellowship with Him forever.

Regardless, death sometimes crashes into our lives hastily, stealing many things we hold dear: people, dreams, security, peace, happiness, and understanding. Such is the case when we lose a child, or when some other tragedy strikes and suddenly snatches our loved one away unexpectedly. In these instances, we overwhelmingly feel that it is *not* time. Words may likely fail us. Our faith may falter, too. So how do we respond in moments like these? How did Jesus?

We know from the last chapter that Jesus got pretty emotional when His friend Lazarus died. When Jesus's own death loomed large before Him, He gathered His closest friends, went to a peaceful place called the garden of Gethsemane, and prayed. He not only prayed, but He poured Himself out at His Father's feet. Jesus allowed His emotions to overcome Him as He metaphorically crawled into His daddy's lap.

> He took Peter, James, and John with him, and he became deeply troubled and distressed. He told them, "My soul is crushed with grief to the point of death. Stay here and keep watch with me."
>
> He went on a little farther and fell to the ground. He prayed that, if it were possible, the awful hour awaiting him might pass him by.
>
> (Mark 14:33–35)

This moment is so critical in the life of Jesus that Luke elaborates on it in his gospel, as well.

> He walked away, about a stone's throw, and knelt down and prayed, "Father, if you are willing, please take this cup of suffering away from me. Yet I want your will to be done, not mine."
>
> Then an angel from heaven appeared and strengthened him. He prayed more fervently, and he was in such

agony of spirit that his sweat fell to the ground like great
drops of blood.

(Luke 22:41–44)

Jesus, too, felt so strongly about death that He was "in agony of
spirit" and sweat "drops of blood." His "soul was crushed with grief."
He prayed for a different outcome, yet submitted Himself to God's
will, regardless of His emotions and questions at the time. Death
doesn't always come sweetly at the end of a long life to a person sur-
rounded by loved ones, as I described in the last chapter. Sometimes
death suddenly and even violently rips a loved one from our lives,
and grief threatens to truly overtake us.

The bottom line is this: Jesus understands our pain. He knows grief, intimately.
If Jesus fell apart when his friend Lazarus
died and when He thought about His own
death, we should know we can fall apart
at such times, too. God can handle our
sorrow, and our Savior can relate to what
we're going through.

*God can handle
our sorrow,
and our Savior
can relate to
what we're
going through.*

I want to share an article I wrote after the untimely passing of
one of my teenage daughter's high school friends. It describes the
kind of grief that comes out of nowhere, changing lives forever.

FOR THE LOVE OF DAVID

The doorbell rang and I got up from the couch where I was
watching a Disney movie with my child who was home sick from
school that day. Opening the door, I saw an elementary-aged
David Palestrant and his mom, Doe Palestrant, our neighbors

on the street behind us.

"Hi!" I exclaimed. "What are you guys doing here? I'm so sorry, but Grace is sick, so I can't invite you inside."

"That's ok," Doe replied. "That's why we're here."

A small, curly-headed David presented a Sonic cup to me with a brightly colored liquid inside. "I heard Grace's throat hurts. I brought her a slush to make it feel better. Will you give it to her for me?"

A simple gesture of kindness from a young boy, served with a genuine and infectious smile.

I will always treasure this memory of David, especially now that the life of this young man was cut tragically short this week due to a car accident, at the age of 17. David was the light of his family's lives. He was the only child of his parents, Doe and Mike. They adopted him from Guatemala. He was their beloved son. David was a member of our church youth group, and he attended youth retreats and gatherings. He loved Jesus. He loved singing and dancing. He loved supporting and encouraging the people he cared about. He loved his friends and family. And he loved being a Tivy Antler.

The last time I saw David, he was riding on a flatbed trailer with the rest of the Tivy High School football team in the annual Homecoming parade. Somehow out of the hundreds of people lining the streets, he saw me and singled me out, teasing me for dropping a piece of ice I was trying to pop into my mouth at the exact moment the team was passing in front of me. I pointed wildly at him and he pointed back at me, then flashed that gigantic smile of his directly at me as the trailer moved out of sight. He had been injured that week and was undergoing surgery the next day, so I messaged him numerous times over the next few weeks to check on him. One of his last messages to me ended with, "Love y'all. Hope the family's good."

Truthfully, the family's not so good right now. Not his family or mine, not his friends' families, not our church family, not his football family, not his Tivy High School family, and not his Kerrville family. When death comes in and rips the life of one of our children from our grasp, we all cry out in anguish.

I wrote in a chapter about facing grief in my book, *Grace-faced,* that we have to experience grief with open hands and not clenched fists.[7] We know, according to Scripture, we are not alone in our suffering.

> *Do not be afraid or discouraged, for the LORD will personally go ahead of you. He will be with you; he will neither fail you nor abandon you.*
> (Deuteronomy 31:8)

But how do we experience God's comfort and presence when we are so weighted down with agony? The answer lies in the body of Christ. God sends His comfort through others. Ordinary people. You and me. The hands and feet of Christ. Jesus with skin on. Every hug, note, smile, meal, ride, flower—every kind gesture—comes from God the Father. When we're in our darkest moments, wondering where God is, we simply need to look around. He is everywhere.

If you are blessed not to be personally affected by this loss, reach out to those who are grieving. Just be present with them, if nothing else. Show up so they know they're not alone. Open your hands to share the comforts of the Holy Spirit. If you are on the painful end of this loss, I encourage you to open your hands as well, to receive the blessings God is sending your way through others. Don't isolate yourself. God can handle all our feelings, even our anger and confusion, so raise those hands to heaven and cry out to your Heavenly Father. He wants to be a part of our process, to comfort us, and to stay in relationship and communication with us.

David was the kind of kid I could always pick right back up with like no time had passed at all, even if we hadn't spoken in a while. He had a special way of being able to have a serious conversation with me, followed by teasing me, and somehow wrap it all up with an impressive degree of respect and manners. He was a special kid.

I write this message, for the love of David. I show up and surround the Palestrant family and the teens in our community in whatever ways I can, for the love of David. I hug my kids a little tighter tonight, for the love of David. I wear my Tivy gear with a little more pride, for the love of David.

And I grieve. Oh, how I grieve. For the love of David.

Sometimes, everything inside us cries out, "It's not time!" This kind of agonizing grief is unfortunately too common in this world, but that means we never have to feel alone while going through it. And when it's too difficult to walk that valley of death in our own strength, praise God that He carries us in His mighty arms.

Live like Jesus

Inside . . .

If death comes like a thief in the night, know you are not alone. Jesus not only understands your pain, but He counts your tears and comforts you in your heartache.

. . . and Out

Using Jesus as an example, what are some ways you can be encouraged in your grief? What are some tangible ways you can support and encourage others who are grieving sudden loss?

At Least There's Coffee

—— *Overcome like Jesus* ——

I woke in the dark of early morning, a full hour before my alarm was set to wake me. I dragged my feet across the cold tile floor and headed to the bathroom where I dipped a cup three times into a bucket of water on the floor. I deposited the icy water into the toilet tank so I could flush it, and chose to ignore the numerous drips that dotted the bathroom tile. I walked slowly to the sink and turned the faucet on to wash my hands, only realizing my mistake after no liquid flowed from the tap. I settled for hand sanitizer.

Despite the warmth in our bedroom and bathroom, I braced myself for the frigid remainder of the house where the heat had been out for days. I sleepily made my way through the poorly lit rooms, flipped the switch on in the pantry, and thought to myself, "Hallelujah! We still have power!" My icy hands fumbled with separating the coffee filters. I looked out the pantry window, shocked at the unfamiliar sight of my frozen front yard looking like the tundra. The eerie silence of the neighborhood was deafening. I poured water from the Brita pitcher into the coffeemaker, and my second clear thought since waking emerged: at least we can make coffee.

A morning with no water in the house can make even the most cheerful person a bit grumpy. Having to go outside in frigid temps for the fourth consecutive day to collect snow and ice in a bucket just to flush the toilets can turn a grumpy person downright grouchy. Some days are harder than others . . . and sometimes, those hard days stretch into hard seasons.

We experienced one of these seasons partly due to Texas's massive winter storm in 2021, which I described above. The storm caused many of the expensive repairs and replacements in our new-to-us home that we had lived in for fewer than six months.

In that period, we replaced: two cracked and leaking toilets; the blower in the main HVAC system; an HVAC unit; a kitchen faucet and supply lines; an outdoor faucet and supply lines and pipes; a compressor on a refrigerator/freezer; all valves and the pump on the water heater; a city water booster pump, twice; an oven; a clothes washer and dryer; a giant stained-glass window that revealed massive wood rot and wood-eating carpenter ants; and a gas grill. We repaired: a broken pipe and well pump; busted lawn sprinklers; an attic vent that was allowing water to seep in and down a bedroom wall; a second leaking upstairs window that sent water dripping from the ceiling downstairs; a laptop and a desktop computer; and dozens of large holes in the exterior of the house where woodpeckers tried to break in and nest. We also treated our beautiful yard for a fungus that was suddenly leaving giant, yellow circles of dead grass in its wake.

We easily could have fallen prey to a pity party, or completely lost our cool like Tom Hanks in *The Money Pit*, but truth be told, we loved our new home, and we praised God for the incredible blessing of living in it. Sometimes, particularly in today's culture, we opt for a martyr mindset and mistake blessings for suffering, rather than tackling our problems head-on and with gratitude. I am often guilty of this myself.

Corrie ten Boom, author of *The Hiding Place*, tells a story of learning to thank God for the fleas that tormented her and her fellow prisoners at Ravensbrück concentration camp during World War II. How could a person be thankful for filthy insects that plagued her with itching and burning, and caused painful scabs and sores all over her body? Because, according to ten Boom, the male guards didn't want to deal with the fleas, so instead of coming in and raping the women at night, the guards stayed away.[8] This may be an extreme example of mistaking a blessing for suffering, but we all know God works in mysterious ways. Corrie ten Boom provides an incredible example of overcoming an obstacle by focusing on a key mindset: gratitude.

> Be thankful in all circumstances, for this is God's will for you who belong to Christ Jesus.
>
> (1 Thessalonians 5:18)

How we choose to view events in the world around us speaks volumes about our faith. Are we simply a pawn—or victim—in others' games? Or, are we a tool in the hands of an almighty God, ready and willing to recognize and join Him in what He's doing here on earth? I dare say it's difficult to identify as both.

> *Either we believe God is at work in our lives and the lives of those around us, or we believe we're just stooges in a game called life.*

Friends, we need to stop "playing the victim." If Corrie ten Boom, in a concentration camp, can accomplish this, we certainly can, too. We cannot possibly conquer the difficulties life will certainly throw at us if we see ourselves as defeated before the battles even begin. As Christians, our testimonies of an all-powerful, all-seeing God are cheapened by followers who constantly whine and complain about how the world is treating us. God never said life would be fair. He never said life would be easy. Either we believe God is at work in our lives and the lives of those around us, or we believe we're just stooges in a game called life. Rest assured that the stooges of this world are not overcomers.

When did we start seeing all the events of the world as an evil, man-made conspiracy against us, instead of seeing the hand of God in the workings of the world? Which testimony will we choose for ourselves? Can we learn to be grateful even for the hardships, trusting God is working for good in our lives?

Jesus already answered this question for us with a resounding "yes," as documented by His disciple, John.

> "I have told you all this so that you may have peace in me. Here on earth you will have many trials and sorrows. But take heart, because I have overcome the world."
>
> (John 16:33)

The world and its problems don't have to take us down, because our Savior already conquered the world. Jesus knew the disciples would have to rely entirely on Him and His teachings if they were to survive the coming persecution following His arrest, crucifixion, and death. Most of us face nothing as dire as what the disciples did, and yet we know from Scripture that amid their imprisonments and floggings and other forms of suffering, these men continued to sing praises to God and preach the salvation of Jesus. Perhaps they didn't ask "Why me?" because they'd witnessed their friend Jesus under similar torture submitting to God's will, even to the point of death.

"O death, where is your victory? O death, where is your sting?"

For sin is the sting that results in death, and the law gives sin its power. But thank God! He gives us victory over sin and death through our Lord Jesus Christ.

(1 Corinthians 15:55–57)

Jesus not only overcame the world; He overcame death itself. Ever since the garden of Eden, sin led to death and separation from God. However, with the sacrifice and resurrection of the promised Messiah, God prevailed in eternal triumph over evil.

Let's ask ourselves: Are our words and actions leading others to Christ—even in times of hardship—and dripping with evidence of the all-powerful God we serve? Or, are we belly-aching and burning in entitlement, putting up barriers between ourselves and non-believers? Do our words and actions draw others to God and make them want to know the Savior we adore? Or, do we project a worldly perspective, lacking in real faith and weakening the idea of an almighty God?

After writing about Corrie ten Boom, Jesus, and the disciples, I feel my beautiful home's repair and replacement drama pales in comparison. The point is not to compare, but to remember, in *all* things, God wants us to trust in His strength and rely on His provision. We are not victims. With the help of Christ, we are overcomers.

Live like Jesus

Inside . . .

When life becomes difficult, is your first response to complain or to reflect on how Jesus has overcome the world and its problems? Think about the testimony of your words and actions. Like it or not, other people are watching and listening to how you respond to life's challenges, and you can either draw people toward God or push them away from Him.

. . . and Out

What are some ways you can point others to God during troublesome times? Identify three specific ways you can practice gratitude during trials, and implement these strategies the next time life gets rough.

"I Belong Here" and Other Mid-Life Delusions

—— *Remain Holy like Jesus* ——

I arrived back at my five-year-old son's school after a morning pre-kindergarten field trip with his class. When the teachers let the children loose on the playground to get out their remaining wiggles, one of my son's sweet classmates walked over to me, cuddled up against my leg, and reached out and grabbed hold of my hand. Seeing this, my son, Johnathan, came racing across the length of the playground screaming, "She's not yours! She's MINE!!"

The part of me concerned with being a great parent felt ashamed at the selfishness and possessiveness of my son. The touchy-feely mama part of me, however, reveled in the "my son loves me and is proud of me" moment.

Flash-forward to the present, with my son now firmly in his teen years, and I remember that moment incredibly fondly. Currently, I'm not even sure he wants his peers to know I'm his mom. No wonder I'm experiencing a mild identity crisis.

I affectionately recall the season of my life when I was completely wrapped up in the all-day, everyday life of raising babies and little children. The "mommy years" were exhausting, but they also afforded me some built-in, tight-knit friendships I clung to for survival. Playdates, mothers' day out groups, music and me classes, tumbling, reading circles at the library—our mommy lives revolved around these tiny humans, and we capitalized on every moment to connect and converse with other grownups in these circles. All those activities for our children also meant an hour here or there for adult conversation and friendship.

For the first time, many of my friends are now experiencing "empty nest" syndrome. They're going out of town every weekend to visit wineries, watch college football games, and visit their grown or nearly-grown children. They reconnect with their college friends and eat lunch while drinking wine with girlfriends.

I have landed somewhere in the middle-ground of no-man's (or no-woman's) land. With a mid-teen, late teen, and baby adult child, I find myself smack dab in the center of *midlife*. I have to say, it's lonely here. Gone are the built-in parent support groups of the mommy years, and not-yet-come is the footloose freedom of the empty nester years. I am a mom of teens, and let me just say, the teen years do strange things to parents.

Well-known for their poor decision-making, teens do stupid stuff their parents don't want to acknowledge to other parents. Teens freak the you-know-what out if Mom proudly posts a picture of them on social media. Teens want their parents to "not be seen" and also "not be heard." And, heaven forbid we parents socialize with our kids' friends' parents; that's an unforgivable sin! No, we sit in our cars in the junior high pick-up lane with our heads down and our eyes on our phones, unwilling to make eye contact with one another for fear our teen will see the social exchange and erupt as soon as he or she enters our vehicle.

It's hard to feel like we are out of place and like we don't belong. God hard-wired us with emotional and spiritual needs for intimacy,

belonging, and connection. He did this so we would need *Him*, but
we mistakenly impress those needs upon
others. Then, we get all tangled up trying
to get our needs met from sources in the
world that were never designed to meet
them in the first place.

> *The truth is, we
> are not supposed
> to belong to this
> world or feel like
> we "fit in" here.*

The truth is, we are not supposed to
belong to this world or feel like we "fit
in" here. We're supposed to be set apart
for God's purposes alone. We're supposed to belong solely to Him.
That's what "holiness" means, and Jesus Himself asks us to be holy.

> But now you must be holy in everything you do, just as
> God who chose you is holy. For the scriptures say, "You
> must be holy because I am holy."
>
> (1 Peter 1:15–16)

What does Jesus's brand of holiness look like in practice? We
can look at the verses that immediately preceded verses 15 and 16
for some ideas.

> So prepare your minds for action and exercise self-con-
> trol. Put all your hope in the gracious salvation that will
> come to you when Jesus Christ is revealed to the world.
> So you must live as God's obedient children. Don't slip
> back into your old ways of living to satisfy your own
> desires. You didn't know any better then.
>
> (1 Peter 1:13–14)

Mentally prepared, self-controlled, obedient, and unselfish . . .
do these adjectives describe us? They're lofty goals. Add to this the
pressure to conform and belong in our contemporary world, and

the task of holiness grows even more difficult.

Years ago, the ancient Israelites struggled with these same concepts. Prone to worship idols, the restrained, agricultural Israelites were easily swayed by pagan worship rituals that offered luxury and sensuality. We're not all that different from them. And yet, God still calls us to be different, holy, and set apart.

> Since you have heard about Jesus and have learned the truth that comes from him, throw off your old sinful nature and your former way of life, which is corrupted by lust and deception. Instead, let the Spirit renew your thoughts and attitudes. Put on your new nature, created to be like God—truly righteous and holy.
>
> (Ephesians 4:21–24)

In practice, being holy like Jesus means living every aspect of our lives in ways that bring glory and honor to our Heavenly Father. Jesus never did anything to shame His Father, God. In all His actions, Jesus submitted to the will of God. As this verse in Ephesians says, we must "throw off our old sinful nature" and "renew our thoughts and attitudes" so we can be "truly righteous and holy."

Jesus knew the pressures to conform—after all, nonconformity cost Him His life—yet He never sinned. He can relate to our struggles, because He had His own temptations and suffering to overcome. Jesus didn't belong, in our traditional sense of belonging, while He was here on earth. He set out to be different and to challenge the current culture. That's because He focused on belonging to God and carrying out God's purposes. No selfishness could be found in Him. Jesus knew the world would mock, disown, and disavow Him, but He went about His kingdom work anyway; furthermore, He did so without compromising His godly character.

He remained holy.

We see the holiness of God and His Son during the transfiguration when Jesus took Peter, James, and John to a high mountain where they also encountered Elijah and Moses. Jesus's appearance changed before the men's eyes, and his face and clothing became radiant like the sun.

> But even as he spoke, a bright cloud overshadowed them, and a voice from the cloud said, "This is my dearly loved Son, who brings me great joy. Listen to him." The disciples were terrified and fell face down on the ground.
>
> (Matthew 17:5–6)

Essentially, God was running towards His son screaming, "He's mine!" May we never doubt for a second, no matter in what phase of life we find ourselves, that Jesus is running toward us screaming, "You're *mine*!" And may we respond boldly and with all holiness, for all the world to see, "and I am *His*."

Live like Jesus

Inside . . .

Recognize that you cannot achieve holiness on your own. Only because of the sacrifice of Jesus and the gift of the Holy Spirit can you even aspire to be holy. Unlike Jesus, you are not perfect. The key is making an effort. And when you succeed, give all credit to your Heavenly Father, in a similar manner to Jesus.

. . . and Out

Only by internalizing the character of Jesus and accepting His love and mercy can you become holy. Spend more time in the Word and prayer. Spend less time focusing on contemporary culture and "fitting in." Aim to please God, not man. Tell God you desire to become more like Jesus in your thoughts, words, and actions. Watch as He honors your prayer and transforms you.

Self–Abasement and Other Critical Mistakes

—— Be Humble like Jesus ——

I slowly got up from the recliner where I had just completed yet another coughing fit and dragged myself into the kitchen where I retrieved my coffee mug. One-third of my morning coffee, now cold, still rested inside the mug. I picked it up and decided to re-warm the coffee, then add more coffee so I could enjoy a full, steaming cup for my scratchy throat. I placed the mug in the microwave, waited for the beep, then took the mug out and placed it on the counter. I retrieved the carafe from the coffeemaker and proceeded to fill the mug. At this point, it dawned on me that I just poured cold coffee on top of my freshly warmed coffee. I said out loud, "You are not the brightest one sometimes, Nicki." Ouch. I instantly recognized the harmful self-talk. I quickly course-corrected with, "But you're sick, so it's okay for now." This was my attempt to offer myself grace, which I try to encourage other people to do for themselves, especially when they are healing from physical, emotional, or spiritual pain.

I used to think chastising myself (like I did when I first realized my coffee mistake) was the same thing as being humble. I'm not sure when I began to confuse humility with self-abasement, but I don't think I'm the only one to do so. Pastor and author Rick Warren said in *The Purpose-Driven Life,* "Humility is not thinking less of yourself, but thinking of yourself less. Humility is thinking more of others."[9] Perhaps this means we should be thinking of our Father in heaven more, as well. Humility is recognizing we are the absolute apple of our Father's eye while also acknowledging we cannot take a single breath unless He grants it to us. It's knowing God would sacrifice His son just to share intimate fellowship with us, and also acknowledging that without Him, we are nothing.

When I think of humility now, I desire to look more like Jesus. We think of Jesus as humble, yet the Bible does not tell us of a time when He criticized Himself, spoke poorly of Himself, or belittled His accomplishments or abilities. For Jesus, humility did not mean disparaging Himself, but it did mean setting aside His own desires so He could serve God. When doing God's work led to moments of applause, Jesus deflected that praise to His Heavenly Father.

> *When doing God's work led to moments of applause, Jesus deflected that praise to His Heavenly Father.*

So Jesus told them, "My message is not my own; it comes from God who sent me. Anyone who wants to do the will of God will know whether my teaching is from God or is merely my own. Those who speak for themselves want glory only for themselves, but a person who seeks to honor the one who sent him speaks truth, not lies."

(John 7:16–18)

"And though I have no wish to glorify myself, God is going to glorify me. He is the true judge."

(John 8:50)

Jesus did not seek accolades for His own sake but only for God. His teachings about humility go far beyond just deflecting praise, though. Jesus spoke about humility on a Sabbath day while He attended a meal in the home of a Pharisee leader. He taught that trying to exalt ourselves can and will result in our downfall.

> When Jesus noticed that all who had come to the dinner were trying to sit in the seats of honor near the head of the table, he gave them this advice: "When you are invited to a wedding feast, don't sit in the seat of honor. What if someone who is more distinguished than you has also been invited? The host will come and say, 'Give this person your seat.' Then you will be embarrassed, and you will have to take whatever seat is left at the foot of the table!
>
> "Instead, take the lowest place at the foot of the table. Then when your host sees you, he will come and say, 'Friend, we have a better place for you!' Then you will be honored in front of all the other guests. For those who exalt themselves will be humbled, and those who humble themselves will be exalted."
>
> (Luke 14:7–11)

God desires to promote only those who do not puff themselves up with pride or self-importance. Jesus continued with His lesson.

> Then he turned to his host. "When you put on a luncheon or a banquet," he said, "don't invite your friends, brothers, relatives, and rich neighbors. For they will invite you back, and that will be your only reward. Instead, invite the poor, the crippled, the lame, and the blind. Then at the resurrection of the righteous, God will reward you for inviting those who could not

repay you."

(Luke 14:12–14)

Beyond deflecting praise or trying to garner acclaim, Jesus addressed our need for humility even while serving others. During the Sermon on the Mount, He reiterated this message that we are to serve others so we can please God, not to please ourselves or the world.

> "Watch out! Don't do your good deeds publicly, to be admired by others, for you will lose the reward from your Father in heaven. When you give to someone in need, don't do as the hypocrites do—blowing trumpets in the synagogues and streets to call attention to their acts of charity! I tell you the truth, they have received all the reward they will ever get. But when you give to someone in need, don't let your left hand know what your right hand is doing. Give your gifts in private, and your Father, who sees everything, will reward you."
>
> (Matthew 6:1–4)

Our motives matter because God sees our hearts. Whether we pursue recognition by performing excellently in our vocations or we seek it by performing visible charitable acts, if we are seeking praise for ourselves, we prove ourselves prideful and not humble. Jesus considers humble service to mean serving others without regard for reward or reputation.

I think I often miss the mark on this completely though, much like the disciples at the Last Supper. Mere moments after Jesus took on the lowest rank of a servant and washed the disciples' feet, they began playing the "who is better than whom" game.

Then they began to argue among themselves about who would be the greatest among them. Jesus told them, "In this world the kings and great men lord it over their people, yet they are called 'friends of the people.' But among you it will be different. Those who are the greatest among you should take the lowest rank, and the leader should be like a servant. Who is more important, the one who sits at the table or the one who serves? The one who sits at the table, of course. But not here! For I am among you as one who serves."

(Luke 22:24–27)

This is how Jesus lived His life, humbly serving others by focusing solely on the kingdom work His Father planned for Him. Rather than seeking pleasure for Himself, Jesus sought to please only the One who sent Him here.

So Jesus said, "When you have lifted up the Son of Man on the cross, then you will understand that I AM he. I do nothing on my own but say only what the Father taught me. And the one who sent me is with me—he has not deserted me. For I always do what pleases him."

(John 8:28–29)

I wish I could say the same . . . that I only say what God has placed in my mouth, and I always do what pleases Him. I am nowhere near capable of this, though. I rely wholly on the Holy Spirit to guide me in my daily attempts to live a life worthy of His calling, because I recognize that humility and obedience are tied closely together.

Jesus knew none of us were deserving of God's love, forgiveness, or salvation. He came and died for us anyway . . . for *all* of us. The ground at the foot of His cross is a level playing field, perfectly even. We all find ourselves in the same position there, kneeling or flat on our faces, in desperate need of a savior. In this way, none of us can boast. On the other hand, how dare we put ourselves down when the greatest man who ever lived chose to die for our benefit? True humility acknowledges we're worth Jesus dying for while also acknowledging we're worthless without Him. That oxymoron may be why humility proves decidedly difficult for us. But if we're ever in doubt, we can follow Jesus's example and deflect praise to God, lower ourselves in service to others, and guard our hearts and motives.

> *True humility acknowledges we're worth Jesus dying for while also acknowledging we're worthless without Him.*

LIVE LIKE JESUS

Inside ...

Who is one of the humblest people you know? What qualities and behaviors do you see in that person? Do you think of yourself as humble? Remember, God sees not only our actions but our hearts.

. . . and Out

Remember to serve others without regard for personal recognition, and if praise or compliments come, deflect those sentiments back to God. Guard your heart and motives by always keeping in mind that everything you are is a direct gift from Him.

Chip Clips and Other Necessities

—— Receive and Offer Peace like Jesus ——

D o not—I repeat—do *not* go to Walmart or Target with your child two days before his or her big move to college. If you are anything like me, that situation—while walking up and down every single aisle in the store—will go down something like this:

"Do you need a blanket? Do you have enough pillows? Do you have ibuprofen and a thermometer? What if you get sick? Oh! Trash bags. You definitely need trash bags. Don't forget to buy some Clorox wipes and dust cloths. Are you set for towels? Look at that—chip clips! You need a chip clip!" I exclaimed, tossing items into the basket.

"Mom, I don't need a chip clip," my daughter said matter-of-factly.

"You totally need a chip clip. I've always had them in the kitchen, but you won't have one. Your chips will go stale after you open the bag. Oh! These are cute! They have little magnets on the back so you can attach them to your fridge. Sweetie, you *need* a chip clip!" I argued.

It was at that moment, as I thrust unwanted chip clips into my daughter's face, that I realized I was not okay. Outwardly, I was busily shopping for her first dorm room; inwardly, I was panicking as I faced an unknown future and a "new normal" for our relationship. I clearly remember a time—I think it was just last week—when she needed me for everything from physical nourishment and comfort to brushing out the tangles in her brownish-blond hair. Today, she needs me to help prepare her for a life lived apart from me. I don't know how to do that.

I've already walked this road with her older sister, but it doesn't make this major life transition any easier. In some ways, it's even harder, because I now know the visits home will get further apart. I know we will remain extremely close, but our relationship will inevitably change. I know she will learn to depend less on me and more on her friends and significant other. I know these next years may be the most fun and exciting times of her life, but I will not be present for the majority of those experiences. I know there will be birthdays and holidays when we won't sit around a table together. I also know all these things are exactly as they should be.

That doesn't mean I'm okay with it, though. It doesn't mean I am at peace.

Whether a parent or not, life is full of crazy twists, turns, and transitions. At times, it feels like the only thing we can do is hold tightly to the roller coaster's lap bar while our hair blows violently behind us and our stomachs drop to our shoes. That's not exactly a peaceful picture. Yet, peace is precisely what Jesus models for us, and what God calls us to, regardless of the unexpected hairpin turns on our ride. True, spiritual peace comes from knowing and trusting Almighty God is with us and in control. Moreover, it comes from accepting Jesus's sacrifice and believing it atoned for our sins, thereby re-establishing peace between God and us.

Jesus demonstrated this to His disciples during a tumultuous night on the water.

Now when they had left the multitude, they took Him

along in the boat as He was. And other little boats were also with Him. And a great windstorm arose, and the waves beat into the boat, so that it was already filling. But He was in the stern, asleep on a pillow. And they awoke Him and said to Him, "Teacher, do You not care that we are perishing?"

Then He arose and rebuked the wind, and said to the sea, "Peace, be still!" And the wind ceased and there was a great calm. But He said to them, "Why are you so fearful? How is it that you have no faith?"

(Mark 4:36–40 NKJV)

It is easy for us to focus on the roar of the wind and the waves, the thunderous sounds and flashes of lightning, and the water filling our tiny lifeboats. Is Jesus with us? If He is, does He care about the storms crashing into our lives? Is He sleeping through our calamities? If He wakes up, is He capable of restoring calm and order? How can we possibly have peace?

Therefore, since we have been made right in God's sight by faith, we have peace with God because of what Jesus Christ our Lord has done for us.

(Romans 5:1)

We have peace because of what Jesus has already done for us. He has already saved us. So, when we find ourselves in a whirlwind like the disciples on the water, our only response is to cry out to Him, the Prince of Peace, just as they did. We have to trust that Jesus holds sway over our situations, and that He can and will bring good from them. More than that though, we need to trust Jesus is near *even in the midst* of our storms.

> "And be sure of this: I am with you always, even to the
> end of the age."
>
> (Matthew 28:20b)

Jesus knew the world would try us—to the point of trying to break us, but He also knew He was God's answer to our problem. He understands the trials of the world because He experienced them Himself; not only that, but He went on to conquer all of those same trials. Through Him, we can do the same.

> For our present troubles are small and won't last very
> long. Yet they produce for us a glory that vastly out-
> weighs them and will last forever! So we don't look at
> the troubles we can see now; rather, we fix our gaze on
> things that cannot be seen. For the things we see now
> will soon be gone, but the things we cannot see will
> last forever.
>
> (2 Corinthians 4:17–18)

Once we learn to receive the peace only Jesus can give us, He expects us to offer that peace to others.

> And let the peace that comes from Christ rule in your
> hearts. For as members of one body you are called to live
> in peace. And always be thankful.
>
> (Colossians 3:15)

> Do all that you can to live in peace with everyone.
>
> (Romans 12:18)

Paul acknowledges we will have cause for complaints against others. People and situations in this world will try to rob us of our peace. As followers of Jesus who have been reconciled to God, though, we are called to extend the peace we enjoy to others. With the Holy Spirit residing inside us, we can experience better control over our words and actions than most unbelievers. Perfect peace is rarely provoked to anger.

Jesus will help us. He is with us. He understands us. Jesus offers us a supernatural peace that transcends our circumstances . . . if we seek to know and abide in Him. Jesus offers us the following reassurance, saying:

> "I am leaving you with a gift—peace of mind and heart. And the peace I give is a gift the world cannot give. So don't be troubled or afraid."
>
> (John 14:27)

We cannot find peace in this world or its circumstances, and we cannot allow ourselves to worry so much about tomorrow's challenges that we are robbed of all the wonderful blessings happening around us today. If we expect the world to provide our contentment, we can't also expect God to provide our peace. Real, lasting peace and contentment can only come from a deep, abiding relationship with Him, the Prince of Peace.

We have to trust that Jesus holds sway over our situations, and that He can and will bring good from them.

Jesus explicitly tells us He has gifted us with peace of mind and heart. The gift is ours to claim. All we have to do is open it, much like that elusive bag of your favorite chips that most definitely needs a cute chip clip.

LIVE LIKE JESUS

Inside...

During trials, do you tend to panic or pray? Do you seek the Prince of Peace or some other form of comfort?

...and Out

Seeking pleasure from the world is a natural response to life's difficulties, but it's not what God wants for us. The next time life feels like it is a roller coaster going off the rails, reach out for the stability of Jesus. Lean into the peace only He can provide.

Surgeries, I.R.S. Fraud, Grief, and a Big "Yes, Lord"

—— Sacrifice like Jesus ——

"I'm being audited by the I.R.S.?" my daughter asked. "How does that happen? I'm only nineteen years old!"

Sure enough, someone stole my barely-an-adult daughter's identity and used it to file false I.R.S. claims. Believe me, the process of proving her identity was long and riddled with anxiety. This experience unfortunately kicked off two weeks' worth of bad news. Next, she learned she needed to have three surgeries during the next two years, two of which required extensive recovery. After that blow landed, she discovered the roommate she had fostered a relationship with and planned room décor with had suddenly been assigned to someone else, leaving Grace to room with a stranger. Then, the university notified her it rejected both her first and second choices of major. So, my sweet girl—while grieving the sudden, excruciating loss of her grandmother—prepared to move away from home for the first time in the middle of this firestorm. During her first week at school, I had to deliver the news her dog was dying from cancer and only had weeks to live.

Right in the middle of this chaos, something extraordinary was also happening. God was calling Grace into ministry. Despite her misgivings, a complete change to her plans, and years of studying and working to be a nurse, Grace responded to God with, "Yes, Lord." Suffice it to say, God was completely rocking her world.

We know we can place our hope in God because He is faithful (Hebrews 10:23), but that doesn't mean saying "yes" to God completely smooths out the road ahead of us. We will face sorrow. We will lose patience. We will fail. We will face injustice. We will be required to make difficult sacrifices. Why should our lives look any different from the life Jesus lived? He faced all of these circumstances as well. Following Jesus comes with a cost. And honestly, if it didn't, it wouldn't hold its value.

> We are pressed on every side by troubles, but we are not crushed. We are perplexed, but not driven to despair. We are hunted down, but never abandoned by God. We get knocked down, but we are not destroyed. Through suffering, our bodies continue to share in the death of Jesus so that the life of Jesus may also be seen in our bodies.
>
> (2 Corinthians 4:8–10)

During His time on earth, Christ learned all about sacrifice. To begin with, He gave up much of His divine privilege when He started life on earth as a human. He could have arrived as the wise, conquering king the Jews expected, full of battle victories, strength, and pride. Instead, He came as a poor, defenseless, knowledgeless newborn, subject to the same circumstances we face. He subjected Himself to the trials of study and learning, respected the authority of His parents and government, and faced the challenges of growing in stature, knowledge, and skill. He could have skipped the experiences of babyhood, childhood, and puberty, but He did not; He endured them for our sake. As a young adult, Jesus gave Himself over to the Temple where He learned from and also taught other rabbis. He forewent the tradition of marriage and its inherent blessings, choosing instead to travel and spend all His time focused on spreading the truth of God and His purpose here on earth. He endured testing by the devil himself, yet He did not cave to temptation or use any of His supernatural powers to make His circumstances easier. Jesus consistently lowered Himself so He could elevate others.

Jesus sacrificed in all these ways and more. We know of His ultimate sacrifice—the giving of His precious life in exchange for our salvation and forgiveness of sins. Have you ever considered the questioning, misunderstandings, and wrong accusations He endured before going to the cross? He chose not to defend Himself nor point the blame elsewhere; He spoke only the truth God had given Him. Next came the physical torment of lashings, beatings, and more. Still, He focused only on His greater purpose. Then came the actual crucifixion. All He possessed as a human—His very life—He sacrificed for us. He gave up everything and expected nothing in return.

Yes, Jesus knows sacrifice. The question is, how do we respond to His generosity? If Jesus's life included so many great sacrifices, what should we be offering from our own lives?

> Then Jesus said to his disciples, "If any of you wants to be my follower, you must give up your own way, take up your cross, and follow me."
>
> (Matthew 16:24)

We should offer everything. God wants all of us, completely and totally surrendered to Him. He wants us to say, just like my daughter did, "Yes, I will do what You are asking me to do, God!" despite our misgivings, upended plans, and questions. God wants us to sacrifice all our thoughts, plans, and ideas and lay them aside in exchange for His plans for us, just like Jesus did. Everything Jesus did and said while walking the earth aligned with God's plan for reclaiming His people. Believe it or not, everything we say and do should, too.

The Gospel of Mark describes an encounter Jesus had with a rich man who asked what he needed to do to gain eternal life. Jesus told the man, in essence, to keep the commandments, and the man replied he had been doing that since he was a young child.

> Looking at the man, Jesus felt genuine love for him. "There is still one thing you haven't done," he told him. "Go and sell all your possessions and give the money to the poor, and you will have treasure in heaven. Then come, follow me."
>
> (Mark 10:21)

The man walked away upset, not sure he could do what Jesus asked of him. You see, Jesus told the rich man to give up his possessions because Jesus knew how much the man's "stuff" meant to him—more than following Jesus meant to him. Jesus will require us to sacrifice any and every thing that stands in the way of our relationship with Him.

> Then Peter began to speak up. "We've given up everything to follow you," he said.
>
> "Yes," Jesus replied, "and I assure you that everyone who has given up house or brothers or sisters or mother or father or children or property, for my sake and for the Good News, will receive now in return a hundred times as many houses, brothers, sisters, mothers, children, and

property—along with persecution. And in the world to come that person will have eternal life."

(Mark 10:28–30)

Remember, following Jesus comes at a cost, and that cost may be persecution. Herein lies the beauty of the economy of God, though. Anything we surrender to Him, He returns a hundred-fold in eternity. I know I am so distracted by so many shiny things this world offers. However, I also know if I can start by surrendering each day to God and asking Him to direct and guide me, then nothing I sacrifice will compare to the fulfillment I will find in doing His will, not to mention the beauty of the life after this one.

Jesus will require us to sacrifice any and every thing that stands in the way of our relationship with Him.

Jesus is no longer here as a human on earth, so we are to be His hands and feet now. We should never forget, though, what Jesus's hands and feet endured. His feet carried the dust of towns where He was rejected and despised. His healing hands were criticized for doing the exact work they were created to do. His hands and feet were pierced by large nails that secured Him to the cross. Being the hands and feet of Christ will come with sacrifices, just as it did for Jesus Himself. But in His faithfulness, God promises the compensation will truly blow our minds, if we simply say, "Yes, Lord."

Live like Jesus

Inside . . .

Have you ever felt God ask you to sacrifice something for Him? Did you follow through? If so, what was the result?

. . . and Out

Remembering that following Jesus comes with a cost, what is something you can sacrifice at the foot of the cross? A comfort, a bad habit, your doubt? Jesus gave His all, and He wants the same from us. Don't hold anything back from Him.

A Nicki by Any Other Name, Would Still Be the Same

—— Know Your True Identity like Jesus ——

B etween the ages of three and four years old, my son experimented with all kinds of names to call me. If his attempts to grab my attention did not yield what he deemed a timely response, he would simply try again with a different moniker. One exchange progressed rapidly from "Mama" to "Mommy," and ended with "Mommy Carlson!" He also enjoyed this game:

"Mommy, what's your name?" he asked.

"My name is Nicki," I replied.

"Nooooo," he countered, "it's Mommy."

"What's your name?" he asked again.

"Mommy," I replied.

"Nooooo," he rebutted. "It's Nicki!"

One morning as he slid out of the car with his oversized backpack dwarfing his preschool frame, I lovingly called out, "Bye, Sweetie!" and he replied, "Bye, Sweetie-Mommy!" So, I melted into a maternal puddle right there in the school drop-off line.

We all struggle to forge our identity in this world. We may answer to many names in the course of our lifetimes: wife, athlete, daughter, boss, sister, teammate, mom, employee, grandmother, or student. The list is endless. Gender, for example, is a critical component of who we are, but the entirety of a person's identity can never be reduced to a single word like "boy" or "girl." Why, then, are we so preoccupied with labeling ourselves and others?

Perhaps we do this because we want to be known and understood. We want others to see and value all the unique stuff on our insides. We all share this need. But, with so many adjectives describing just one person, it's no wonder we long to connect with our true identity. There are many facets to our personalities, but none can describe us in our entirety. We may perform many duties, but who are we, really? And better yet, who do we *want* to be?

Jesus never questioned His identity as the Son of God, the Messiah, and the long-awaited Savior. Furthermore, He didn't feel the need to prove this fact to others, which was yet another sign of His humility. Even in the face of tremendous persecution and pain while hanging on the cross of crucifixion, Christ remained true to His identity and His mission.

> The leading priests and teachers of religious law also mocked Jesus. "He saved others," they scoffed, "but he can't save himself! Let this Messiah, this King of Israel, come down from the cross so we can see it and believe him!" Even the men who were crucified with Jesus ridiculed him.
>
> (Mark 15:31–32)

We know Jesus refused the temptation to prove Himself in the face of these insults, because we know He remained on the cross, despite having the ability to save Himself. This doesn't mean Jesus didn't feel the physical pain of the crucifixion, because, despite His divine nature, Jesus was human in His physical form. Jesus was so certain of His identity, though, that He felt no pressure to prove it to anyone.

When Jesus was brought before the Council to answer questions relating to His identity and behavior, He waited to answer until they asked Him straight-forwardly if He was the Son of God.

> But Jesus was silent and made no reply. Then the high priest asked him, "Are you the Messiah, the Son of the Blessed One?"
>
> Jesus said, "I AM. And you will see the Son of Man seated in the place of power at God's right hand and coming on the clouds of heaven."
>
> (Mark 14:61–62)

Ask yourself this: If you met a stranger on the street, would he or she need to know Jesus before being able to know *you?* In other words, is your identity so woven together with Christ that no one can recognize or understand who you are, without first knowing Him?

Jesus asked His disciples to tell Him just who they thought He was.

> When Jesus came to the region of Caesarea Philippi, he asked his disciples, "Who do people say that the Son of Man is?"
>
> "Well," they replied, "some say John the Baptist, some say Elijah, and others say Jeremiah or one of the other prophets."
>
> Then he asked them, "But who do you say I am?"
>
> Simon Peter answered, "You are the Messiah, the Son of the living God."

> Jesus replied, "You are blessed, Simon son of John,
> because my Father in heaven has revealed this to you.
> You did not learn this from any human being."
>
> (Matthew 16:13–17)

I want to proclaim who Jesus is every chance I am given. I want to so closely identify with Christ that when others look at me, they see Him. I want to project the love, mercy, and grace of Jesus Christ in all my interactions. Wanting and doing are remarkably different things though, and I know I come up very often, very short of this goal. I may desire to imitate Christ, but if I am not spending time daily in God's Word and in prayerful conversation with Him, my life will reflect more of a chaotic state like that of Nicki, rather than resembling the life of Jesus. We cannot identify with our Heavenly Father and His Son unless we intimately know them. Like any relationship, this requires time and devotion.

I want to so closely identify with Christ that when others look at me, they see Him.

> Yes, everything else is worthless when compared with
> the infinite value of knowing Christ Jesus my Lord. For
> his sake I have discarded everything else, counting it all
> as garbage, so that I could gain Christ.
>
> (Philippians 3:8)

Today, when I read Paul's description in this verse that he "discarded everything else, counting it all as garbage," I ask myself if I can do the same. Can I count all the other labels the world fixes on me as trash? Honestly, I'm pretty fond of some of them: Friend. Sister. Wife. Mother. Author. But if I lost them all, I know I would still cling unwaveringly to the most important one: Jesus follower.

Paul faced quite an identity change himself. Once a noticeably vocal and active member of the legalistic Jewish Pharisee sect, he prided himself on persecuting those who broke Jewish law, including early disciples of Jesus. After meeting Jesus on the road to Damascus though, Paul completely changed his identity and life's work—to that of "Christ follower." I dare say anyone who has an intimate encounter with the Lord will find it difficult to remain unchanged.

One night at bedtime my son informed me he wanted to change his name. He said, "By the way, Mom, you can call me Mr. Pee-Pee Poopy Pants." I assumed I had a *Captain Underpants* book to thank for this impromptu declaration. Then my son reassured me, "That's not really my name, Mom." I replied, "I know, kid. I named you."

Our identities should be so rooted in Jesus Christ that even a name change won't phase us. All else should pale in comparison to this one identifier. I need to remember I am not called to be anyone except the person God created me to be. Since there's only one "me," that must mean I'm not called to be like anyone else . . . except Christ.

We are to love and accept—no, embrace—others' unique identities, just like Jesus did.

If we want to be our best selves, we must strive to be our most *authentic* selves. Our identities are unique because God created only one of each of us. Miraculously, in true God-mysterious-fashion, we somehow simultaneously share our most important identity though—children of God and followers of Christ. We are all different, and yet the same.

Regardless of the proverbial hats we currently wear or have worn in the past, we can all long for a future in heaven where our identities are no longer tied to our accomplishments or titles. Though we hunger for our new identities in heaven, we know He has work for us here on earth. Our job is to share His message of love and redemption as far and wide as we can, just like Paul did, for as long as we draw breath here. We are to love and accept—no, *embrace*—others' unique identities, just like Jesus did.

> But we are citizens of heaven, where the Lord Jesus Christ lives. And we are eagerly waiting for him to return as our Savior.
>
> (Philippians 3:20)

Let's plant ourselves in the knowledge that, just like Jesus, we share dual citizenship on earth and in heaven. Let's root ourselves in our identities as children of God and followers of His Son, regardless of the many other names to which we may answer here on earth.

Live Like Jesus

Inside ...

Jesus modeled the importance of knowing who (and whose) He was, without demanding everyone recognize and revere Him. What steps can you take to adopt this attitude for yourself?

... and Out

Make a conscious effort not to label others. When we attach group identifiers to individual people, we generalize all aspects of who those people are, and we fail to account for their many unique differences and traits. It's easy to demonize a group (because that's an ideology), but it's much more difficult to demonize a singular, complex individual. While we're at it, let's stop labeling ourselves as well. Leave room to be *all* the beautiful things God entrusted within you. Only one label matters in the end anyway: follower of Jesus Christ.

Live Like Jesus on the *Outside*

Now that we have internalized the character of Jesus, we will begin to see a change in the way we live our lives. Thinking and feeling like Jesus is not enough; now, we must *act* like Him. We must learn to speak, react, and interact like our Savior did when He walked the earth. If Jesus were here now in the flesh, how would His life look? If we want to live like Jesus, we must resemble Him on the outside through our actions as well as on the inside.

Where's My Fire?

—— *Worship like Jesus* ——

The Christmas Eve candlelight service is one of my favorite worship services of the year. I cherish the cold outside, the warmth inside, the family members far and near coming together, the anticipation of the birth of the Messiah, and the familiar carols of Christmas sung with emotion and nostalgia.

One particular Christmas Eve, my husband and I stood at the front of the church singing a heartfelt rendition of *Silent Night* while the symbolic light of the world began spreading—one hand-held candle at a time, row by row, from the back of the church. Our children sat near the front of the room with family members and friends of ours while my husband and I led worship. The youngest of our crew, Johnathan, was a busy three-year-old at the time, and I could see him clutching the white candle with the paper wrap in his tiny hands, like a prize. As the adults on either side of him passed the flame over him, and as we continued to earnestly lead *Silent Night*, our son exclaimed with increasing volume and frustration, "Where my fire?" . . . "Where MY fire?" . . . "WHERE MY FIRE?!!"

Our friends and family found it impossible to maintain straight faces and soon succumbed to loud fits of laughter, audible to the entire congregation. My husband and I tried in vain to stifle our "church giggles," overcome our parental embarrassment, and continue singing the sentimental song that concluded the service. We re-tell this story every Christmas to this day.

We cannot expect a three-year-old to maintain focus throughout an hour-long church service, particularly one with fire, candles, and Christmas trees. But what about the rest of us? Is our worship lacking the passion and sincerity God desires from us? Are we distracted? Where is *our* fire for God? If we were to worship like Jesus did, how would that look?

Dr. Constance Cherry, a worship professor, writer, and leader, says the following about Jesus in a blog titled *Worship like Jesus*:

> He was a worshiper from birth who consistently, even daily, worshiped at the Temple and the synagogue, kept the Sabbath, spent much time in prayer, participated in the regular worship rituals, worshiped God in defiance of Satan, read the Scriptures in the synagogue service, cleansed the Temple, celebrated the Jewish annual festivals of worship, pronounced blessings upon people, sang the liturgy, preached, and taught in the Temple and synagogue.[10]

When it came to worship, Jesus wasn't reinventing the wheel. He participated in corporate, historical, traditional worship and rituals. However, what we learn about worship from Jesus is still substantial. In the Old Testament, *who* the Israelites worshiped (Almighty God alone) and *where* the Israelites worshiped (in the Temple and the Promised Land) were the primary focuses. This geographic requirement meant Jews traveled great distances, numerous times a year, through hostile territories, just to worship God in His Temple. In the New Testament, Jesus explains this geographic requirement (the *where*) has changed to an internal location. Through the gift of the Holy Spirit, God now resides inside each of us, meaning we can worship Him whenever and *wherever* we choose.

> Jesus replied, "Believe me, dear woman, the time is coming when it will no longer matter whether you worship the Father on this mountain or in Jerusalem. You Samaritans know very little about the one you worship, while we Jews know all about him, for salvation comes through the Jews. But the time is coming—indeed it's here now—when true worshipers will worship the Father in spirit and in truth. The Father is looking for those who will worship him that way. For God is Spirit, so those who worship him must worship in spirit and in truth."
>
> (John 4:21–24)

In this verse, Jesus teaches us that how and where we worship means nothing if we are not sincerely and wholeheartedly focused on God. Worshiping in spirit and truth means God desires our actual souls to adore Him. The meaning of this message goes far beyond the words Jesus spoke, though, because it also matters to whom Jesus was speaking. He was talking to a Samaritan woman. Now, a man teaching a woman was scandalous enough, but this woman was from the hated lands of Samaria, and Jews and Samaritans did not associate with one another—at all. Jesus's unspoken message was that He was about to fling wide open—for *all* people—the doors for worshiping the one true God ... even for women and Samaritans.

Our worship reflects our thoughts about the object of our devotion, so when our self-focused desires begin making themselves known while we are worshiping, we need to recognize we are no longer worshiping the Creator—we are worshiping the created. When it desperately matters to us with whom we sit, where we sit, the color of the pew and carpet, the nature of the person's sin across the aisle from us, and the style and specifics of the music being played and sung, we have completely missed the mark. God wants no part of that kind of "worship."

> "I know all the things you do, that you are neither hot nor cold. I wish that you were one or the other! But since you are like lukewarm water, neither hot nor cold, I will spit you out of my mouth!"
>
> (Revelation 3:15–16)

The point of the practice of religious worship is not to make us feel good or to check a "to-do" off our "good Christian" list. The point of worship is to bring us closer to God in mind, spirit, and action because only He is worthy of such attention. The prophet Isaiah also addressed this.

> "What makes you think I want all your sacrifices?" says the LORD. "I am sick of your burnt offerings of rams and the fat of fattened cattle. I get no pleasure from the blood of bulls and lambs and goats …
>
> Stop bringing me your meaningless gifts; the incense of your offerings disgusts me! As for your celebrations of the new moon and the Sabbath and your special days for fasting—they are all sinful and false. I want no more of your pious meetings …
>
> When you lift up your hands in prayer, I will not look. Though you offer many prayers, I will not listen, for your hands are covered with the blood of innocent victims.

Wash yourselves and be clean! Get your sins out of my sight. Give up your evil ways. Learn to do good. Seek justice. Help the oppressed. Defend the cause of orphans. Fight for the rights of widows."

(Isaiah 1:11,13, 15–17)

Obedience to religious tradition is meaningless if our hearts are not engaged in the routine. God doesn't want us to simply "go through the motions" of going to church and Bible study. The real, meaningful worship God craves from us comes when we crawl off the throne of control and honor in our own lives and place Him on that throne where He belongs. When we do this, God can then direct us to the kingdom work at hand: doing good, seeking justice, and helping the oppressed. All these, when done with a pure and sincere heart, are acts of worship, too.

> *Obedience to religious tradition is meaningless if our hearts are not engaged in the routine.*

When my son desperately longed for his candle to be lit during that Christmas Eve service, the object of his worship had obviously shifted from God. Sometimes we find ourselves longing for a temporary spark rather than the eternal flame of the Holy Spirit. Our fiery feelings during religious worship should reflect a consistent passion and focus on the Creator, not the created. May we learn to worship in spirit and truth with our entire souls devoted to God, just like Jesus.

LIVE LIKE JESUS

Inside . . .

Have you ever considered what your worship means to your Heavenly Father? How do you think your worship makes Him feel? What kind of things commonly take your focus and attention off of Him?

. . . and Out

Take time to prepare your heart and mind for worship. Get quiet and still. Focus your mind on God. Pray. If you find yourself in a "worship rut," sit somewhere else. Attend a different service. For one week, go to a different church. Worship by seeking justice, caring for the oppressed, and serving those in need. When we enter into worship—any form of worship—and we are prepared for the experience, God is faithful to meet us there.

Naked and Unafraid

—— Love like Jesus ——

I clearly remember a morning in which I was quietly getting ready for the day when my son burst into the bathroom saying, "You can't answer the door naked, Mom! You have to put clothes on first."

I looked down, confused by the clothes covering my body, and asked, "Is there someone at the door, Johnathan?"

He replied, "No, I'm just sayin'." As he said this, he gestured flippantly with both of his hands and knocked my mug out of my grasp, spilling coffee all down the front of my fully-dressed self and all over the floor.

Ten minutes late now (and donning a new outfit), I navigated the morning traffic to drop him off at school, all while my exasperated mind wondered if I would ever emerge from this always-something-unexpected-at-the-last-minute kind of life. We said goodbye and I love you, and I watched as he walked away from me all by himself, his tiny body struggling with the weight of his backpack and the heavy door to the school. I thought to myself, "I hope we never do emerge from this crazy stage of life, but I sense it's coming sooner than I'd like."

I was mostly correct. Already gone are the days of helping him get dressed and packing his backpack for him, and here now are the days of making sure he's eaten something and knows where he's left his car keys. Mornings are still a little crazy—or truth be told, grumpy—with this child, but goodness, I love my son so very, very much.

For most parents, this is an obvious statement, and a comment so common we may gloss right over it while reading, without pausing to let the meaning of those words penetrate our hearts and minds. The same thing can happen when we *say* those three little words.

For me, right now in this moment, just typing those words brings actual tears. You see, love—the biblical, 1 Corinthians 13 kind of love— is a risky business. To love another person unconditionally is to take one's own heart and place it on an altar of sacrifice, just like Abraham did with his son, Isaac, and just like God did with His son, Jesus. To truly love means to willingly take a chance on incredible pain and torment . . . actual

> *God didn't intend for us to love with expectation. He wants us to love with intention and action.*

heartbreak. Why? Because God didn't intend for us to love with expectation. He wants us to love with intention and action.

This weekend, my husband and I plan to drive our son to a nearby city so he can meet—in person—his birth family. We have no idea how this meeting will unfold. Some of my friends and prayer partners keep asking me how I feel about all of this, and I reply that I'm not overly concerned with my feelings . . . only with my son's feelings. How will *he* process the myriad of emotions this encounter will bring forth? Will this heal and bring peace to some of the deep hurts within his soul, or will it inflict new and more damaging wounds? All I know is I will support—rather, *love*—him through it all, with no regard for my own heart. No expectation of return, just intention and action.

Biblical love leaves a person completely vulnerable. Despite the great risk, it also carries the potential for the sweetest rewards this side of heaven. For me, I've had the incredible blessing of watching God perform miracle after miracle in my son's life. I've had the privilege of holding my son's hand while he underwent medical tests, when he took his first steps, when he went to school for the first time, when he learned to pray, and when we grieved deep loss together. I've had a front-row seat to every joy and disappointment in his sixteen years of life. I've been the serendipitous recipient of all of his "I love you, Mommy!" and "Mommy, where are you?" and "Mom, can you come pick me up?" moments. And I wouldn't trade them for anything in the world. Love holds the power of transformation, both of the loving and the loved.

> *My adopted son taught me that love transcends blood, inheritance, and entitlement, and is instead a precious, unearned gift.*

My adopted son taught me that love transcends blood, inheritance, and entitlement, and is instead a precious, unearned gift. No expectations, only intention and action. He also taught me that to love others as God loves us, we must love with open hands, hearts, and minds, not with tightly closed embraces. I could easily wrap my arms around my son right now and refuse to let him meet his birth family, but doing this would be for my own sake and heart's protection, not his. And that's simply not how love operates. Love looks outward to others. Love is selfless.

I could write an entire book about the one topic of loving like Jesus does. But the main point I want to get across is this: God *is* love. And He loves *us*. And we demonstrate our love for Him by loving *others*. God's love forms a perfect, never-ending circle.

> Dear friends, let us continue to love one another, for love comes from God. Anyone who loves is a child of God and knows God. But anyone who does not love does not know God, for God is love. God showed how much he loved us by sending his one and only Son into the world so that we might have eternal life through him.
>
> (1 John 4:7–9)

No person who has ever walked this earth has loved more completely, selflessly, unconditionally, and sacrificially than Jesus. The way He accomplished this was not by *speaking* those three little words. No, Jesus *lived out* His love—with intention and action. Jesus's love moved Him to do things like washing his friends' feet, healing lepers, feeding hungry people, fellowshipping and eating with renowned sinners, and suffering to the point of death on the cross. To put it another way, love made Jesus give up His comfort and put others first—to *serve* them.

I am bothered by all the popular memes and social media conversations about how "Jesus didn't hang out with sinners to condone their sin, but rather to transform their lives." This statement may be true, but I feel it misses the mark. Jesus hung out with sinners because He truly loved them. His first intent was simply to love; transformation was a response, or byproduct, of that perfect love. Furthermore, only God's sacrificial brand of love holds that power of transformation. We are not

Our job is to love as unconditionally as we can and leave matters of transformation up to God.

capable of that. Our love is but a poor reflection of the perfect love we've been given, because we are sinful, broken people. Sometimes our love can hold enough shock and meaning to prompt some change in another person, but even that change is prompted by the Holy Spirit, not by us. So, to focus on transformation in others is to "put the cart before the horse," as my grandparents would say. God, in His great love for us, sent His son to die on our behalf *while we were yet sinners.* Our job is to love as unconditionally as we can and leave matters of transformation up to God. We can't do that if we've pushed Him out of the judgment seat and decided to take up residence there ourselves. Our job is to love as closely to God's perfect love as possible, and it is His job to do the rest.

> "So now I am giving you a new commandment: Love each other. Just as I have loved you, you should love each other. Your love for one another will prove to the world that you are my disciples."
>
> (John 13:34–35)

> We know how much God loves us, and we have put our trust in his love. God is love, and all who live in love live in God, and God lives in them.
>
> (1 John 4:16)

So, I say take the risk. Love intentionally. Love actively. Love vulnerably. Love selflessly. Love bravely, deeply, and generously. Love openly and blatantly. Love "nakedly and unafraid." Love transformatively. Love like Jesus.

LIVE LIKE JESUS

Inside...

Think of a person who made you feel truly loved, and note what behaviors and actions they exhibited. Do you portray these same characteristics in your love for others?

...and Out

We all need love, but some of us have a greater need than others. Pray for God to open your eyes to see someone who needs Jesus's brand of love. With intent and action, try to offer the love of Christ to that person. If you haven't already, start inside your own home and family.

I'm Sorry, But I'm Not Here Right Now

—— *Fellowship like Jesus* ——

O ur little family of five sat around the table eating the simple supper I had prepared. Inevitably, as we began sharing about our day and excited little voices began interrupting each other, the phone rang. My husband, John, got up to check the number and, seeing it was unfamiliar, declined to answer it. So, our too-quick-to-catch four-year-old son, Johnathan, hopped down from his booster seat, picked the phone up off its receiver, and said, "Hello?"

We watched as he stood there, silently listening, for a few seconds. He had never answered the phone before, but we assumed it was an automated message and returned to eating. Then Johnathan, whose legal name is John, pulled the phone from his ear and said, "They want John Carlson."

I said, "Tell them you *are* John Carlson," and snickered. But my husband responded, "Tell them I'm not home."

Johnathan returned the phone to his ear and said matter-of-factly, "I'm not home."

We all erupted into laughter as the phone line went dead. Johnathan laughed hysterically, despite not understanding his double-meaning joke.

Telemarketing calls are an unwelcome addition to any meal or time of fellowship. People, on the other hand, should always be welcomed—or better yet, invited. Jesus was a masterful example of hospitality and welcome, and table fellowship played a critical role in His ministry.

In her book, *The Gospel on the Ground*, author Kristi McLelland speaks to the significance of biblical examples of table fellowship. "Eating together was one of the highest values in the ancient Jewish world and still is today throughout the Middle East. Whom you ate with said everything about you—it was your affiliation with them. Whom you ate with symbolized whom you welcomed, embraced, and accepted."[11] In other words, eating together was an act of fellowship.

It stands to reason then, that if we want to fellowship like Jesus, we should look at the people with whom He ate. Examples from the book of Luke tell us Jesus enjoyed table fellowship with sinners, tax collectors, a "sinful woman," and Pharisees.

> Later, Levi held a banquet in his home with Jesus as the guest of honor. Many of Levi's fellow tax collectors and other guests also ate with them. But the Pharisees and their teachers of religious law complained bitterly to Jesus' disciples, "Why do you eat and drink with such scum?"
>
> Jesus answered them, "Healthy people don't need a doctor—sick people do. I have come to call not those who think they are righteous, but those who know they are sinners and need to repent."
>
> (Luke 5:29–32)

Much to the surprise of the religious leaders and Israelites, Jesus didn't come to fellowship with them or the organized church. He came to seek out and save the lost. Arguably, His favorite place to do that was around a table, eating and drinking. Jesus modeled what God's table looks like, and—surprise—it's not an exclusive supper club or a "Who's Who" affair. It's an open-to-all, come-as-you-are, no-shame-in-this-game, open invitation. Jesus doesn't say we need to get ourselves right with God before coming to Him. Jesus doesn't say we need to have all the answers and be free of doubt before coming to Him. Jesus doesn't say we need to look, speak, and act perfectly before coming to Him. Jesus doesn't even say we need to believe exactly like denominations x, y, or z tell us we should believe before we come to Him. He simply says, to *everyone*: Come. Sit. Eat. Drink. Let's talk.

> *Jesus modeled what God's table looks like, and—surprise—it's not an exclusive supper club or a "Who's Who" affair.*

In the early days of the church, the disciples continued Jesus's approach to fellowship, and their number of followers grew exponentially.

> They worshiped together at the Temple each day, met in homes for the Lord's Supper, and shared their meals with great joy and generosity— all the while praising God and enjoying the goodwill of all the people. And each day the Lord added to their fellowship those who were being saved.
>
> (Acts 2:46–47)

I think the present-day American church is largely failing to offer and experience fellowship this way. How can we expect newcomers to walk through church doors we've already closed to them?

We want to tell everyone exactly how to think, how to vote, and how and what to believe before they ever cross the threshold of our churches' doors; and, if people don't line up with our ideas, we label them "sinners" and tell ourselves we're being righteous by calling them out for their moral corruption. Never mind the sin in our own lives. Never mind the fact that salvation and conviction of sin are wholly under the realm of God, His Holy Spirit, and His son Jesus—not us. Never mind the fact that these outsiders, desperate for God's love and salvation, now have no clue how divine love looks or feels, because it was our job to embody it for them.

If the church as an institution rejects sinners and excludes them from the free and open fellowship of the kingdom of God, and if it keeps them from serving and leading, who will be left to worship God? No one. Because we are *all* sinners. That is why the Lord's table is open and welcome to *all*. Jesus did not come in judgment but as an invitation to salvation and abundant life.

> God sent his Son into the world not to judge the world,
> but to save the world through him.

(John 3:17)

Our job is to simply bring people to the table where they can feast on God's goodness, and allow God to do the work of bringing them to repentance and salvation. It's not our job to be God! We forget this truth and allow our religious practices and traditions to get in the way of God's message of love and redemption through Christ. We need to stop acting like we have everything all figured out. We can't peer down our noses and point fingers at those who aren't playing the game the way we want them to, or who are not agreeing with us on all the issues we feel are important. When we think and act this way, it's all too easy to decide "those people" are wrong and quite simply "not one of us." It all begs the question: Are

> ### *Are we guilty of excluding from Christian fellowship the very people Christ Himself sought to include?*

we guilty of excluding from Christian fellowship the very people Christ Himself sought to include?

When our religious or cultural practices become barriers or obstacles that harm others' relationships with God or that hinder their access to church community and fellowship, they prove to be human-made stumbling blocks that don't originate from God. The narrative of the Bible consistently shows us that relationship with us—*all* of us—is always His goal. Such judgment and condemnation from Christ's followers only damages how others view Him. The "I'm right and you're wrong" attitude only impedes our ability to draw others to God's table. The "I'm against *that*" philosophy translates into "I'm against *you*," and it effectively closes the door on those starving for the bread of life.

We cannot love the comfort of our homogenous fellowship more than we love others or more than we love Jesus Himself. Welcoming others to Jesus's brand of fellowship looks like kindness, not criticism; acceptance, not ridicule; forgiveness, not condemnation; servanthood, not privilege; and invitation, not exclusion.

As the familiar saying goes, when we find ourselves with more than enough, we should build a longer table, not a higher fence. When it comes to your table, is your message to the outside world that you're not home? Or, is your door open and the food plentiful, with empty seats just waiting for someone hungry to come and eat?

There is plenty of room at the Lord's table, so slide over and invite someone new to the feast.

LIVE LIKE JESUS

Inside . . .

When church-goers hear the word "fellowship," they tend to think of gathering together with like-minded people, eating a potluck lunch, or going on a community outing as a group. Jesus's brand of fellowship looked a lot more like outreach than in-reach. Have your thoughts about fellowship changed since reading this chapter? If so, how?

. . . and Out

When was the last time you invited someone outside of your regular circle—not a friend or family member—into your home for a meal? How about a church service? Look for an opportunity and get busy offering Jesus's kind of fellowship to those in need around you.

Words and Other Weaponry of Life and Death

—— Teach like Jesus ——

I hold a vivid, snap-shot memory of my daughter, Grace, sitting on the floor of the kitchen with her pre-school-aged brother, Johnathan, teaching him to tie his shoes. I remember her hot pink tank top and her blondish-brown hair falling into her eyes as she leaned over to help him. Her kindness and patience with her brother's tiny toddler fingers that fumbled clumsily with the laces just mesmerized me. When one method proved too difficult for him and he grew frustrated, she consoled him by saying, "It's okay, Johnathan. Watch again, and I'll show you a different way." My teaching attempts with him had not worked, so I gratefully accepted her help. Sure enough, with practice and patience, she successfully taught him to tie his shoes.

I remember my oldest daughter, Rachel, bent over notebook paper and worksheets with Johnathan, re-teaching mathematical concepts he struggled to understand. As his body wiggled and his agitation mounted, Rachel tried one approach after another until she landed on one that "clicked" in his young mind. If a teaching method confounded him, she abandoned it and tried another. Without fail, the little light bulb of understanding turned on, and then they would celebrate their mutual success.

My sweet girls never condemned their brother for not knowing how to tie his shoes, for not learning fast enough, for not trying it the way they told him to, or for having black laces instead of white ones. I think we, as Christians, often try this condemnation-style approach when teaching others, especially when it comes to teaching biblical concepts. We try to teach through accusation and shame, rather than with patience and love like my daughters.

When Christians wield the Word of God like a weapon and use it to cut others down, it breaks my heart. I think it breaks Jesus's heart, too. What are we hoping to teach people with this kind of behavior: how to criticize, insult, and demean others with our self-righteous attitudes and criticism? Transformation comes through relationships, not through anger, lecturing, or accusations. We need to ask ourselves what we want to teach others about God, because our actions will preach our most memorable sermons, not our words.

> *We need to ask ourselves what we want to teach others about God, because our actions will preach our most memorable sermons, not our words.*

Again I say, don't get involved in foolish, ignorant arguments that only start fights. A servant of the Lord must not quarrel but must be kind to everyone, be able to teach, and be patient with difficult people. Gently instruct those who oppose the truth. Perhaps God will change those people's hearts, and they will learn the truth.

(2 Timothy 2:23–25)

If anyone had the authority to wield the Word of God like a

weapon, it was Jesus, the Word made flesh (John, chapter 1), but we never see Jesus respond this way when questioned. The Pharisees and other religious leaders of the day tried incessantly to catch Jesus misquoting the Torah or breaking the law, but He always returned their fire calmly, truthfully, and patiently. If Jesus returned to earth, would we expect to see Him in seminary classrooms debating with the smartest scholars of the Bible today? Would we find Him discussing how to live life with the most popular preachers in America? I don't know, but He did spend time discussing religious ideas with Jewish rabbis at the Temple. When it came to the heart of His ministry years though, Jesus spent a great deal of His time teaching basic truths to common people in everyday situations.

Jesus taught everywhere He went, to anyone who would listen, in simple stories (parables) about concepts everyone in His world would immediately understand. The point of parables was not just to tell a story, but to teach a lesson that would result in the listener taking some kind of action or making some kind of change. Jesus didn't make His points by shouting, cajoling, or condemning His listeners. He didn't try to outsmart someone questioning Him, even though the Pharisees used this approach to try to entrap Him on numerous occasions. Instead, Jesus taught by pointing to God and His character, and by showing the path to abundant life.

He masterfully adapted His teaching methods to the situation and audience He wanted to reach. For example, sometimes Jesus removed Himself and a small group of followers from a crowd to talk to them more intimately and at length. We see this in Jesus's Sermon on the Mount in Matthew, chapter 5. In this case, Jesus instructed His listeners through parables and by citing ancient lessons and re-teaching them in new and different ways, like a lecturer.

He also used repetition of phrases in the Beatitudes—the "blessed are" section—to help His listeners better recall the message.

We see another type of Jesus's teaching when He encountered the woman at the well. This is a classic example of Jesus taking advantage of what we moms like to call a "teachable moment." These moments occur naturally when a situation presents itself and a greater lesson can be learned from it. In this story, Jesus is traveling through Samaria and stops at a well where a Samaritan woman is drawing water. He asks her for a drink—an astonishing act, because Jews and Samaritans didn't mingle in Jesus's time, men and women didn't speak in public, and rabbis never deigned to teach or preach to a woman. Jesus's behavior confuses her, so she questions why He has asked her for a drink.

> Jesus replied, "If you only knew the gift God has for you and who you are speaking to, you would ask me, and I would give you living water."
>
> (John 4:10)

Jesus used a question-and-answer technique to reveal the truth to the Samaritan woman slowly, in a way she could discover for herself. He already knew—but still asked her about—her personal life, and He was certainly familiar with her culture and its norms. Instead of ignoring these issues, Jesus used them to His advantage to gain her full attention and pique her curiosity. Jesus also drew an analogy from the task the woman was performing (drawing water at a well) to Himself as the promised Messiah. He used the physical objects and experiences right in front of them to teach this woman a spiritual lesson. Note that Jesus did not enter into this interaction loudly preaching, proclaiming His divinity and righteousness, or shaming the woman for her sin or for not instantly recognizing Him. Jesus used a soft, merciful, uncomplicated approach to teach the Samaritan woman at the well her value in God's eyes.

We see yet another teaching method from Jesus when He set up real-life experiences to get His message across through activity. We see an example of this during the Last Supper, where Jesus uses the meal to foreshadow His death and resurrection to the disciples. He also washed the disciples' feet at this meal, an experience He used to teach about serving others.

> After washing their feet, he put on his robe again and sat down and asked, "Do you understand what I was doing? You call me 'Teacher' and 'Lord,' and you are right, because that's what I am. And since I, your Lord and Teacher, have washed your feet, you ought to wash each other's feet. I have given you an example to follow. Do as I have done to you."
>
> (John 13:12–15)

Would Jesus's message of service to others have been as impactful and memorable had He just told the disciples, "You should serve one another"? Of course not. As the disciples watched the Messiah kneel before them, washing the grime off their feet like the lowest of the servants, they had to wonder what in the world Jesus was doing and why. Before He even spoke a word, Jesus primed each person to hear His intended lesson.

I desperately want patient, practical, and affirming teachers like Jesus and my daughters in my life. I also truly want to serve as that kind of teacher for others, particularly when it comes to the Word of God. I don't invoke the Word to prove a point but to hopefully lead others into a deeper relationship with God. Instead of using our words and the Word as weapons, maybe—if we keep Jesus's teaching methods in mind—our words can show others the way to abundant and eternal life, just like He did.

Live like Jesus

Inside...

Recall one of your favorite teachers. It's easy, isn't it? Teachers make a lasting impression on us. How can you adopt some of your favorite educator's traits into your own life, especially when you are trying to teach others?

...and Out

Remember, your actions are the loudest, most memorable sermon you'll ever preach. Teach the character of Christ to others . . . and only when necessary, use words. Again, if you haven't started this practice within your household, this is where you should begin.

Running Through Sprinklers

—— Study like Jesus ——

One night in late spring, following a worship rehearsal, my young son and I headed for our car in the church parking lot. As we exited the air-conditioned building, a wave of hot air assaulted us. School was not yet out for summer and standardized testing loomed in the coming days. I heard the familiar spraying sound of automatic sprinklers and smelled the wet concrete of the sidewalk. I looked at my son and momentarily remembered the giant task I had just asked of him, to sit relatively still and quiet for the last hour while I practiced with the band. I grabbed his hand, jerked my head toward the sprinklers, kicked off my shoes, then looked back at him and asked, "Wanna run through them?" His gigantic, blue eyes shot up in surprise, and then we took off running across the grass, giggling and chasing one another. We raced through the water numerous times, and I will never forget it. For just a moment, I prioritized fun over the school-day bedtime schedule and routine, and it felt great. Schoolwork and baths could wait.

I haven't always found it easy to put other things ahead of studying. With a staggering need to please and a pressing desire to make the highest grades, school became a bit of an idol for me. So, when I ponder the importance of study in Jesus's life, I find the need to balance the subject with a healthy dose of realism. Christ—God incarnate—studied the Word. That's enough for me right there. Let's look at some concrete examples from Jesus's life.

Jesus prioritized time spent worshiping and learning about His Heavenly Father. We can see this from the time Jesus was a child.

> Every year Jesus' parents went to Jerusalem for the Passover festival. When Jesus was twelve years old, they attended the festival as usual. After the celebration was over, they started home to Nazareth, but Jesus stayed behind in Jerusalem. His parents didn't miss him at first, because they assumed he was among the other travelers. But when he didn't show up that evening, they started looking for him among their relatives and friends.
>
> (Luke 2:41–44)

The Passover festival was one of three "foot" festivals the Jewish people celebrated annually. Families from all over the region would make the pilgrimage to Jerusalem, mostly on foot, to worship God and remember all He had done in their collective past. Jesus's family attended these festivals every year, signifying that worshiping God in traditional and customary Jewish ways was important to them.

In addition to worship, Jesus also prioritized learning about God from religious leaders and experts. While Mary and Joseph were traveling home from the Passover festival, they realized Jesus was not with them. Jesus had stayed behind at the Temple, His Heavenly Father's house, and continued to study and learn from the rabbis there.

> When they couldn't find him, they went back to Jerusalem to search for him there. Three days later they finally discovered him in the Temple, sitting among the religious teachers, listening to them and asking questions.

All who heard him were amazed at his understanding and his answers. His parents didn't know what to think.

"Son," his mother said to him, "why have you done this to us? Your father and I have been frantic, searching for you everywhere."

"But why did you need to search?" he asked. "Didn't you know that I must be in my Father's house?"

(Luke 2:45–49)

A subsequent verse (verse 52) explains Jesus "grew in wisdom and stature and favor with God," offering evidence that God honors our pursuits to know Him better. If the Son of God Himself emphasized study, we can place a safe bet that we can benefit from doing likewise.

Another verse in Luke offers further evidence Jesus studied the Word of God.

When he came to the village of Nazareth, his boyhood home, he went as usual to the synagogue on the Sabbath and stood up to read the scriptures.

(Luke 4:16)

Going to the synagogue on the Sabbath "as usual" implies Jesus did this growing up. The synagogue is where Jewish children went to school to learn the Torah. Most knowledge of Jewish history and religion was passed down orally, so memorization of the Torah was of utmost importance. This is why Jesus often began teaching by saying, "As it is written, . . ."

God honors our pursuits to know Him better.

because this signified to His audience that He was teaching from a place of authority and knowledge of the ancient texts, and they would know whether or not His reference was accurate.

We see this same priority for study and time with God in another encounter in Luke—the story of two sisters named Mary and Martha. Jesus and His disciples were traveling to Jerusalem when they stopped at Martha's home. As was customary for a woman in their culture at this time, Martha began busily preparing a meal for the travelers.

> Her sister, Mary, sat at the Lord's feet, listening to what he taught. But Martha was distracted by the big dinner she was preparing. She came to Jesus and said, "Lord, doesn't it seem unfair to you that my sister just sits here while I do all the work? Tell her to come and help me."
>
> But the Lord said to her, "My dear Martha, you are worried and upset over all these details! There is only one thing worth being concerned about. Mary has discovered it, and it will not be taken away from her."
>
> (Luke 10:39–42)

The words Luke chose to describe what Mary chose to do had specific meaning to the Jewish people. Luke says Mary "sat at the Lord's feet," which was how the *talmid*—or students—of Jewish rabbis were described. While the rabbis taught on the steps of the Temple, their students—all of whom were male, of course—sat at their teachers' feet, soaking in the lessons. Mary, a woman, was learning from Jesus, like a student from a rabbi. This kind of rabbi-to-talmid learning went beyond cerebral knowledge to encompass actions and entire lifestyles. Jesus was showing by His actions that

He welcomed women to study and learn from Him.

The hospitable Martha, trying to uphold cultural and traditional gender norms to bring honor to her family, had neglected the opportunity to sit at the feet of the Savior and learn from Him. Jesus said Mary had made the better choice, and nothing could take the benefits of that choice away from her.

We cannot expect to live like Jesus if we don't closely examine His life. Jesus Himself studied in an attempt to better understand His Heavenly Father, and we need to do the same. If we want to know God, all we need to do is look to His son, for He embodied the nature and character of His Father.

Studying the Lord does not need to feel like a rigorous task or challenge to make a good grade. Think of it as a late spring adventure of running through sprinklers. Look to Jesus, take hold of His hand, and race across the cool grass, getting soaked in His love and mercy. I promise we won't forget the experience with Him . . . or the lessons He teaches us.

LIVE LIKE JESUS

Inside . . .

Do you spend time weekly, or even daily, studying the Word of God? When you neglect this practice, how does it affect you?

. . . and Out

If Jesus needed to study, obviously we do, too. Corporate study, in particular, allows us to learn from others and can only increase the rate of our learning. If you are not part of a Bible study group, I highly encourage you to join one. Many are offered online and through apps if you are unable to attend one in person.

Welcome Home!
I Burned Your Supper

—— *Encourage like Jesus* ——

Near the end of a particularly difficult day that consisted of bad news from doctors, dog messes at home, forgotten items at school, running late to a meeting, incessant sibling bickering, and more, I set about the task of making supper for my family. Despite following the instructions—which implicitly stated the pan should be *searing hot*—the expensive tuna steaks I bought as a surprise for my husband burned in an instant while smoke filled the kitchen. Of course, it was at this hectic and humiliating moment—with smoke billowing from the house, children crying and fighting in the distance, and teriyaki dripping down the front of my dress—that my husband walked through the door.

"Hi, Honey!" I hollered over the vent hood's exhaust fan. "Welcome home!"

I loudly tossed the smoking skillet into the sink and declared, "I burned your supper!"

At this, my husband walked over to me, wrapped me in his arms, and said . . . nothing. He just hugged me for a long minute. When he finally relaxed his embrace, he calmly asked, "What kind of pizza do you want me to order?"

I must say, John truly encouraged me that evening. I felt seen, understood, empathized with, and supported. We often think of encouragement as a smiley-faced cheerleader jumping up and down on the sidelines, yelling optimistic phrases like "You can do it," but that's just shiny stimulation. Biblical encouragement, and the kind of encouragement my husband offered me, looks a little different. If we want to encourage others like Jesus did, we have to be willing to get dirty. Why? Because Jesus encourages us by reaching down to us in our mess, sin, and shame, and lifting us to a high place of honor. Biblical encouragement is not pie-in-the-sky positivity, but found-in-the-ground redemption.

Jesus demonstrated this numerous times in His encounters with women, as told in the Gospels. Why would women need to be encouraged by Jesus? Because in His time, the church and culture had reduced women to a place of subservience. Women were viewed as less than, untrustworthy, and dishonorable. Jesus sought to *restore* women with His encouragement.

> *Biblical encouragement is not pie-in-the-sky positivity, but found-in-the-ground redemption.*

In the story found in Matthew 9 of the woman with the issue of bleeding, Jesus responded to this desperate woman—exiled from her family, friends, and church for twelve years for being "unclean" due to a bleeding issue—with more than just physical healing.

> A woman in the crowd had suffered for twelve years with constant bleeding, and she could find no cure. Coming up behind Jesus, she touched the fringe of his robe. Immediately, the bleeding stopped.
>
> "Who touched me?" Jesus asked.

Everyone denied it, and Peter said, "Master, this whole crowd is pressing up against you."

But Jesus said, "Someone deliberately touched me, for I felt healing power go out from me."

When the woman realized that she could not stay hidden, she began to tremble and fell to her knees in front of him. The whole crowd heard her explain why she had touched him and that she had been immediately healed.

(Luke 8:43–47)

When this woman reached out to touch the corner of Jesus's garment, He did not kill—or even shun—her as the applicable customs demanded. Instead, He turned toward her to truly see her. He physically healed her. He spiritually healed her by crediting her faith. Then, He restored her to full life and standing in her community. That is restoration.

Jesus turned around, and when he saw her, he said, "Daughter, be encouraged! Your faith has made you well." And the woman was healed at that moment.

(Matthew 9:22)

Jesus told the woman to "take heart," or "be encouraged." That's biblical encouragement. Jesus didn't ignore her, withhold His divine mercy, or say, "You'll be okay! Just keep fighting," or "Maybe this is just your cross to bear. I have mine, too. Good luck!" That would be worldly encouragement. No, Jesus went numerous steps further and offered this woman the encouragement of complete and total restoration.

If we want to encourage like Jesus, we first must find people truly in need of encouragement, even if that means going to dark, scary, or uncomfortable places—both physically and emotionally. We must offer compassion, empathy, and understanding, and we must offer them without judgment or criticism. As Jesus did with the bleeding woman, we must do what's merciful, not what contemporary culture expects from us.

Jesus shows us another example of sacred encouragement in His encounter with the woman about to be stoned for adultery.

> "Teacher," they said to Jesus, "this woman was caught in the act of adultery. The law of Moses says to stone her. What do you say?"
>
> They were trying to trap him into saying something they could use against him, but Jesus stooped down and wrote in the dust with his finger. They kept demanding an answer, so he stood up again and said, "All right, but let the one who has never sinned throw the first stone!" Then he stooped down again and wrote in the dust.
>
> When the accusers heard this, they slipped away one by one, beginning with the oldest, until only Jesus was left in the middle of the crowd with the woman. Then Jesus stood up again and said to the woman, "Where are your accusers? Didn't even one of them condemn you?"
>
> "No, Lord," she said.
>
> And Jesus said, "Neither do I. Go and sin no more."
>
> (John 8:4–11)

Jesus's brand of encouragement not only restores—it rescues. It finds the one—not *despite* being guilty of sin, but *because* of it—who needs saving the most. If we could achieve sinlessness on our own, we wouldn't need a savior. Somehow though, we tend to demand others justify their "worthiness" of our help or encouragement. Are they in this mess because of their own mistakes? Well, then, they're "paying the price" now and they "probably deserve it." What have they done to show they're truly sorry, like changing their behavior? If nothing, then too bad for them because they're "just not ready to be helped."

> *Jesus's brand of encouragement not only restores—it rescues.*

Jesus did not ask any of these questions of the woman about to be stoned, and she had been caught *in the very act* of adultery. Her guilt was not in question. Also note, Jesus did not engage with the crowd of accusers and try to reason with them. He simply reminded the crowd that they, too, were sinners just like the adulterous woman; for this reason alone, the mob had no justification for throwing a stone at her. Jesus encouraged the woman by rescuing her and offering her a life focused on Him, rather than on her sin.

Biblical encouragement is much more than a positive attitude shared with others. People need bolstering for everything from burning someone's supper to experiencing devastating grief and loss.

> Until I get there, focus on reading the scriptures to the church, encouraging the believers, and teaching them.
> (1 Timothy 4:13)

Just like Jesus, our brand of encouragement should reach out, rescue, and restore. God wants us to draw near to the hurting, come alongside them in their suffering, and show them the hope of abundant life lived in Him. And that, my friends, is highly encouraging.

Live like Jesus

Inside...

Have you ever found yourself in need of biblical encouragement? When you find yourself in this kind of need, return to the Bible and read some of the stories of Jesus's interactions with women. Rest in the knowledge that Jesus wants to restore and rescue you as well.

...and Out

The next time you encounter someone in need of true encouragement, remember to offer it in the same way Jesus would. Try to identify and—if possible—meet that person's deepest needs. Then, go beyond cheery, simplistic words of reassurance, and instead offer the life-giving wisdom and promises of our Heavenly Father.

A Stone's Throw Away

—— *Suffer like Jesus* ——

The scorching summer sun in Texas rendered it too hot to play outside. As a stay-at-home mom with three young children, I realized an afternoon movie on the couch for the two big kids while the toddler napped meant I could get some housework accomplished. The girls agreed on an animated coming-of-age tale involving friendship, bravery, humor, and of course, animals.

I walked through the living room with a laundry basket on my hip not even twenty minutes into the movie and found my youngest daughter with a sorrowful look on her face and crocodile tears filling her eyes. I said, "Baby! What is wrong?" She sobbed, with tears falling freely down her cheeks now, "They're being *mean* to him, Mommy! Why would they do that? Why?"

Still to this day, this middle child of mine champions the causes of justice and mercy, and her heart bleeds for the mistreated. She absolutely cannot abide by suffering of any kind. I decided a long time ago I wanted to be more like her when I grew up. She advocates for the marginalized in our society and around the world, and sometimes, she feels the heat for it. She is often the target of ridicule due to the causes she fights for and the people she represents. Her grandparents feared she would leave home and others would take advantage of her in some awful way, but those comments only fueled her passion. She may be tender-hearted, but this girl of mine refuses to be called "weak," "naïve," or "vulnerable."

I recently read a quote by Pastor Stan Mitchell that made me think of this daughter of mine, and it stopped me in my tracks. Mitchell said, "If you claim to be someone's ally but aren't getting hit by the stones thrown at them, you're not standing close enough."[12]

Suddenly, I—the one partially responsible for raising this open-hearted and open-handed child—began questioning my behavior. I mean, I agree with these stances my brave daughter takes, but do others know? Because if they did, I would probably be the subject of some of the same ridicule she faces. In other words, am I suffering for others' sake, or just my own? Do I feel the sting of the injustice others are enduring? More specifically, am I suffering like Jesus?

We discussed in a previous chapter, *Fellowship like Jesus,* that Christ aligned Himself at fellowship tables with the most marginalized groups in society. He ate with the lowest of the low. When we align ourselves with marginalized groups like Jesus did, we share in their suffering. We can't be supportive and still "keep our hands clean." Offering mercy is not an easy or sanitary business.

> For God called you to do good, even if it means suffering, just as Christ suffered for you. He is your example, and you must follow in his steps.
>
> (1 Peter 2:21)

When we think about suffering, all too often we think of it in one of two ways: a consequence for our sin or an unfair but natural consequence of living in this fallen world. In both cases, our focus is on us. When Jesus suffered though, it wasn't about Him at all. His focus was on others. Jesus's suffering held a purpose: to reveal the character of God to a world in need of salvation. Our suffering holds purpose as well. One reason God allows painful circumstances in our lives is that when our hearts break wide open, we inadvertently give Him access to come and make a home inside the rubble of our souls. At our weakest points, God offers His strength and comfort.

Let's take a look at one example of Jesus's suffering, which came during His testing in the wilderness, following His baptism.

> Then Jesus, full of the Holy Spirit, returned from the Jordan River. He was led by the Spirit in the wilderness, where he was tempted by the devil for forty days. Jesus ate nothing all that time and became very hungry.
>
> (Luke 4:1–2)

I can't imagine going without food for *four* days, much less *forty*. I cannot fathom that degree of weakness and hunger, but Jesus knew it intimately. At His physically weakest point, the devil tempted Him to turn rocks into bread and eat, to worship him and in return receive all the kingdoms of the world to rule over, and to throw Himself from a high place and prove His deity by not being harmed. Jesus refused in every trial, guaranteeing His continued anguish. He didn't do this for His own sake. He did this to show us how we, too, can withstand temptation.

Jesus's suffering held a purpose: to reveal the character of God to a world in need of salvation. Our suffering holds purpose as well.

During His ministry years, it's no surprise Jesus focused His efforts on "the least of these" —lepers, Samaritans, women, tax collectors, widows, orphans, children—these were the outcasts, the unseen, the neediest, the most despised, or the ones lacking basic rights during Jesus's time on earth. How many stories do we read in the Bible of how He reached out to individuals in these groups, healing them, touching them, forgiving them, and fellowshipping with them? Jesus was determined to reach out to those His culture deemed undeserving of time or attention, and that conviction earned Him a great deal of suffering. Jesus suffered for these same people—the sinners we all are—to the extreme of a merciless beating, humiliating crucifixion, and torturous death on a cross. Aligning His divine self with us cost Jesus His life.

Lest we think the job is done, though, Jesus instructs us to follow in His footsteps. That must mean suffering is our "cross to bear," too. We see this in the lives of His closest friends, the disciples. Paul was beheaded. Peter was crucified. Other disciples were tortured, stabbed, crucified, imprisoned, clubbed, and burned to death.

Are we so influenced by the sacrifice of Jesus and His teachings that we wear targets on our backs the way His early disciples did, or do we try to float under the cultural radar just enough to escape such torment? Maybe, if we're a Christian only when it's convenient or beneficial to us in some way, we're not a Christian—or "Christ follower"—at all.

One reason God allows us to struggle is so we can help others who are struggling. The same applies to suffering. Paul addressed this in his second letter to the church in Corinth.

> All praise to God, the Father of our Lord Jesus Christ. God is our merciful Father and the source of all comfort. He comforts us in all our troubles so that we can comfort others. When they are troubled, we will be able to give them the same comfort God has given us. For the more we suffer for Christ, the more God will shower us

with his comfort through Christ.

(2 Corinthians 1:3–5)

If we do align ourselves with Jesus, we must also align ourselves with the people He reached out to and aligned Himself with—the poor, widows, orphans, adulterers, and tax collectors, for example. Or, to use contemporary terms, we should join the suffering of the homeless, immigrants, addicts, homosexuals, transsexuals, and sex industry workers and victims. If we succeed at this, we should feel the pelting of the stones, because plenty of people are out there heaving them upon these ostracized members of society. We can't harden our hearts, look away, or wish someone else would do something to help, and we can't truly be supportive from a "safe distance" away.

> *Social justice issues reveal where we are failing as a church to be Christ for others—failing to be servant-minded, humble, welcoming, comforting, and merciful.*

Is your back bruised by the rocks, or are you a stone's throw (or safe distance) away? Or, worse yet, are you busy throwing stones?

When a segment of our world is crying out in pain, we need to pay attention. Social justice issues reveal where we are failing as a church to be Christ for others—failing to be servant-minded, humble, welcoming, comforting, and merciful. If we are truly following Jesus, I think He is leading us directly to those who are hurting most. Not only does Jesus want us to see, love, and offer assistance, but He expects us to *join them* in their suffering, just as He did for us.

Live like Jesus

Inside...

What are some reasons you believe God allows suffering? Do your reasons align with what you believe to be the character of God? In what segments of the world's population do you see great suffering? Where do you see suffering in your own neighborhood?

...and Out

Thinking of that specific group or groups from the last question, how can you act—like Jesus did—as a better advocate or ally for these suffering people?

Nicki-bird, Vernie-bird, and Uncle Pasquale

—— Offer Mercy like Jesus ——

"Nicki-bird! Where are you?" called the familiar voice of one of my favorite grown-ups. I ran to the front door and into the long arms of one of my dad's closest friends, Verne. "There she is!" he exclaimed, his giant hug quickly evolving into rib-tickling.

I knew the rules of this tickling game, as we played it often. He would tell me, "Say 'Uncle Pasquale' and I'll stop! Say 'Uncle Pasquale!'" All of this made me laugh so hard that it was nearly impossible to squeak out those crazy words all in one breath. As soon as I could utter them though, Verne would immediately stop tickling me. As a child, I never questioned why he did this, but as an adult, I realized he was teaching me to trust him. I knew he would offer the reprieve as soon as I called for it because that's what he always did.

I also recall a popular game from my childhood that did not involve the same level of trust I had with my Vernie-bird, as he liked to be called. Few childhood games came as close to causing real physical harm as did a little game we called "Mercy." In this so-called game, two kids face one another and put their hands together palm-to-palm, lacing their fingers together at the top. When the game starts, both players try to bend their opponent's hand backward to the point of causing enough pain that the other player concedes defeat by shouting "Mercy!" The victor is supposed to release the other player's hands at this point, but we all know kids . . . and in most cases, the victor enjoyed holding out for a few seconds post-mercy-call to truly humiliate the loser and would sometimes even twist the loser's hand to the side and forcefully downward to bring the loser to his or her knees.

I hated this game as a child. More often than not, I could not rely on the other player to offer mercy when I called for it. Also, I hated anything that causes another person pain. I thought the game should be called "Torture" or "Wrist Wrestling" instead of "Mercy."

According to Compassion International, our word *mercy* derives from the Latin words *merced* and *merces,* meaning "price paid," and it carries the connotation of "compassion, benevolence, kindness, and forgiveness."[13] In these and many other ways, Jesus constitutes our idea of what mercy is and how it should look in action.

One example of Jesus's mercy, in addition to compassion, involves the healing of two blind men. According to the Gospel of Matthew, Jesus left Jericho and was traveling with a large crowd following Him when He encountered two blind men sitting beside the road. The men cried out to Jesus, begging Him for mercy, but the crowd tried to silence them.

"Be quiet!" the crowd yelled at them.

But they only shouted louder, "Lord, Son of David, have mercy on us!"

When Jesus heard them, he stopped and called, "What do you want me to do for you?"

"Lord," they said, "we want to see!"

Jesus felt sorry for them and touched their eyes. Instantly they could see! Then they followed him.

(Matthew 20:31–34)

Jesus not only heard the men's desperate pleas, but He stopped what He was doing and turned towards them. Then, He asked them what they wanted from Him. Jesus didn't ask this in the way a perturbed Mom with toddlers crying for attention might ask. He asked in a love-personified, light-of-the-world kind of way. Jesus asked in a "How can I help you, my friends and brothers?" way.

The men asked for healing of their eyes, so they could see. Jesus restored their sight, exactly as they had asked. The New Living Testament translation says Jesus "felt sorry for them," but the New International Version says He "had compassion on them."

Remember the story of the woman caught in adultery who was about to be stoned? For me, it is one of the most impactful stories of Jesus offering mercy, in addition to forgiveness and encouragement. Let's dive a little deeper into this story as it relates to mercy.

According to the Gospel of John, on the first day after the Festival of Tabernacles, Jesus returned to the Temple to teach. While there, some teachers of the Law and some Pharisees brought a woman before Jesus that they had caught in the act of adultery. Per usual, these Pharisees tried to trap Jesus into contradicting the Torah, an instructional part of the Mosaic Law.

"Teacher," they said to Jesus, "this woman was caught in the act of adultery. The law of Moses says to stone her. What do you say?"

(John 8:4–5)

Jesus responded by drawing in the dirt, careful not to write elsewhere because it was unlawful to do so on this, a Sabbath day. What did Jesus write? We can't be sure, because the Scriptures do not include these facts. Biblical historians propose He may have drawn a "line in the sand" or quoted a verse from the Law concerning adultery.

> They kept demanding an answer, so he stood up again and said, "All right, but let the one who has never sinned throw the first stone!"
>
> (John 8:7)

Following this statement, Jesus again stooped down to write in the dust. Perhaps this time, He wrote other commandments from the Law, or maybe even wrote the names of some of the woman's accusers, or maybe He wrote the name of the man who—according to the Law—should have been facing the same death penalty she was facing. We don't know for sure. The result was startling, though. One by one, presumably while each was recognizing his sin, the men began to walk away, until only the woman and Jesus remained.

> Then Jesus stood up again and said to the woman, "Where are your accusers? Didn't even one of them condemn you?"
>
> "No, Lord," she said.
>
> And Jesus said, "Neither do I. Go and sin no more."
>
> (John 8:10–11)

This exchange gives me life. Does Jesus recognize the woman's behavior as sinful? Yes, He does. Does He excuse it? No, He does not. Does He condemn, exact punishment, or ridicule her for that sin? Also no. So, just how does this work?

Let's approach it another way. God is holy and cannot overlook sin. It has to be called out, and it requires atonement. According to Mosaic Law, the price for sin is a blood sacrifice. Now, I believe Jesus, in His great mercy, would have stepped in front of those stones and kept them from striking and killing her, had that been necessary. Why wasn't it necessary? Because Jesus knew *He* would complete the required blood sacrifice for her *on the cross*.

The Torah was intended to protect God's people, draw them nearer to Him, and show them the way to abundant life. Over time, as the Israelites began following these rules and regulations, they became legalistic with themselves, God, and one another, and it proved a stumbling block in those same relationships. But then, Jesus entered the scene. In everything Jesus said and did, He upheld the Torah, all while also adding to its purpose, meaning, and application.

Mind-blowingly, Jesus manages to teach us a lesson on mercy in this story on two fronts: that of the sinner and the accusers. He contends for us like He did for this sinful woman. He covers us like He covered her. He pays the cost. Also, Jesus contends with the accusers. Does He want or ask for a blood sacrifice for the woman's sin? No. Neither should we when others sin! But the Torah required it, so Jesus accomplished the bleeding for us. *He atoned for us all.* We are not to judge or condemn others for their sin. What right do guilty people have to condemn others who are also guilty? Only Jesus was innocent and capable of throwing a stone, yet *He didn't.* True mercy occurs when the person holding all the power withholds punishment and condemnation and instead offers compassion and kindness.

Finally, what did Jesus ask for in the wake of this woman's acquittal? He said, "Go and sin no more." He asked for *transformation*. God sees our sins. Jesus paid the price for our sins. He does not condemn us for our sin, but instead invites us into a relationship with Him in which sin will no longer have dominion over us. He invites us into the kind of abundant life only He can offer us. If that isn't the most beautiful definition of "mercy," then I don't know what is.

> *True mercy occurs when the person holding all the power withholds punishment and condemnation and instead offers compassion and kindness.*

The merciful standard of Jesus may look like an impossible measure to many of us, so let's break it down into some practical steps. First, pray for eyes to see and ears to hear others the way Jesus did. We can't offer mercy to those in need if we don't acknowledge their needs in the first place. Second, recount the many times we received mercy in the face of rightful punishment or condemnation. If nothing else, try paying them forward. Third, follow Jesus's example. When in doubt, always offer mercy in the form of compassion, benevolence, encouragement, kindness, and forgiveness.

Henri Nouwen said, "Compassion asks us to go where it hurts, to enter into the places of pain, to share in brokenness, fear, confusion, and anguish. Compassion challenges us to cry out with those in misery, to mourn with those who are lonely, to weep with those in tears. Compassion requires us to be weak with the weak, vulnerable with the vulnerable, and powerless with the powerless. Compassion means full immersion in the condition of being human."[14]

We need to listen for the cries of "Uncle Pasquale" in the world, because they're all around us. Have mercy on us, most merciful Father, and help us extend that mercy to others.

Live like Jesus

Inside . . .

Which story illustrating the mercy of Jesus resonated with you the most, and why? Recall an example from your own life of a time you were offered mercy instead of condemnation, ridicule, or punishment.

. . . and Out

We all need mercy. We can add to the crowds demanding recompense for others' mistakes and shortcomings, or we can refrain like Jesus and realize none of us are innocent. The next time you are ready to condemn another person for his or her sin, remember the woman caught in adultery, drop your stones, and walk away . . . just like Jesus did.

Fiery Hot Tears of Injustice

—— *Flip the Tables like Jesus* ——

The familiar squeak of tennis shoes on asphalt and the pop of balls hitting racquet strings filled the sweltering, humid air at the junior tennis tournament. I was still in elementary school, and my dad was running this tournament like he did every summer. My big sister was old enough to compete now, but I was still too young. Despite my age, my mother gave me the shared, yet privileged responsibility of running the Coke trailer. I was living every little kid's dream, drinking all the ice-cold soda my stomach could handle. I can still taste the waxy, paper Coke cups with that syrupy, fountain drink inside. It was hot and sweaty inside that metal trailer, but at least we were in the shade and diving into the ice compartment regularly. My mom gave me instructions about keeping my voice low so I wouldn't disturb matches nearby, and to use my best manners with customers, as I was a reflection on my father, the tournament director/tennis coach.

Everything went well until a couple of bigger kids came in to "help" my friend and me. Before I knew it, they were throwing ice at one another, running around, and squealing. My mother stalked over to me and, in mere seconds, pulled me by the arm into the one and only women's bathroom stall. She lectured; I bawled. She angrily spoke of her disappointment in me; I pled my complete innocence. Never once did I imagine she would think I was guilty, or worse yet, that she *still* wouldn't believe in my innocence after I explained I was not participating in the other kids' shenanigans. She didn't care. I was completely overcome with frustration, but my tears and agitation only solidified her stance.

This memory burns in my mind to this day. I remember vividly my fiery hot tears, my absolute desperation for my mother to believe I hadn't betrayed her trust, the injustice of my firing from the Coke trailer, and my relegation to sit on the grass beside Mom's lawn chair—bored—for the rest of the day. At the same time, the guilty parties continued to drink all the Cokes they wanted, throw ice at one another, and play. My little heart experienced outrage and injustice for the first time. Life had suddenly proven itself horribly unfair.

I realize in hindsight what a small slight I actually experienced, but at the time, my emotions could not be quelled. My overwhelming need for truth and justice outweighed all else. It reminds me of the many times we see Jesus passionately acting on behalf of those same ideals. Jesus exerted great effort to bring justice and righteousness to those most in need, and He did this amid religious and cultural standards expecting—demanding, even—He do the exact opposite. Jesus took expectations and turned them on their heads. He came to make things right, and in doing so, He flipped some tables.

Our first story is a literal example of Jesus flipping tables in the Temple.

> Jesus entered the Temple and began to drive out all the people buying and selling animals for sacrifice. He knocked over the tables of the money changers and the chairs of those selling doves. He said to them, "The

scriptures declare, 'My Temple will be called a house
of prayer,' but you have turned it into a den of thieves!"

(Matthew 21:12–13)

We often hear people use this example of an "angry Jesus" to justify their own angry behavior. We also see this verse used as an example of Jesus's "righteous anger" at the treatment of God's holy Temple. It's important to note, however, that righteous anger requires *righteousness*, which none of us can attain on our own. The point of righteous anger is to point others to God, not to condemn them.

If we take a deeper look at this encounter, we learn Jesus was not just upset about the presence of the money changers and salespeople in the Temple; rather, He wanted to cleanse the Temple of what these people *represented*: unfairness and injustice. Jesus was angry because these people were limiting others' access to the Temple and therefore God. Which people benefitted from the practice of buying and selling animals for sacrifice, and the currency exchange? Only the people offering it. Who paid the exorbitant prices, lost money in the exchanges, or failed to afford the prices altogether?

Jesus took offense and flipped the tables on the people taking unfair advantage of others.

It was the people who traveled great distances to the Temple, who didn't speak the same language, who were not well-versed in mathematics, and who were poor; in other words, the foreigners, uneducated, and marginalized. The people who could not afford the prices were relegated to staying outside the Temple altogether. He wasn't just mad about the wheeling and dealing because it was happening in His Father's home. Jesus took offense and flipped the tables on the people taking unfair advantage of others.

We see another example of Jesus flipping tables in Luke 7:26-50 where Luke tells the story of Jesus going to the home of Simon, the Pharisee, to eat a meal. In Middle Eastern culture at this time, the guests would recline around the table while people of lower station would sit or stand along the wall of the room, hoping for leftovers or scraps at the meal's conclusion. A "sinful" woman sat in this position near the feet of Jesus, weeping loudly over Him, and then she took down her hair and used it to wipe her tears from Jesus's feet. She also poured expensive perfume from an alabaster jar on His feet, anointing Him as a guest of special honor.

Simon, the host, responded to the woman's outrageous and culturally forbidden actions.

> When the Pharisee who had invited him saw this, he said to himself, "If this man were a prophet, he would know what kind of woman is touching him. She's a sinner!"
>
> (Luke 7:39)

Jesus responded by telling a story illustrating how the depth of a person's love and gratitude for a savior is directly proportionate to the debt that person has been forgiven. This woman, for example, exhibited great passion for Jesus because He'd forgiven her great sin debt. What Jesus said and did next, though, proved even more scandalous.

> Then he turned to the woman and said to Simon, "Look at this woman kneeling here. When I entered your home, you didn't offer me water to wash the dust from my feet, but she has washed them with her tears and wiped them

with her hair. You didn't greet me with a kiss, but from the time I first came in, she has not stopped kissing my feet. You neglected the courtesy of olive oil to anoint my head, but she has anointed my feet with rare perfume.

"I tell you, her sins—and they are many—have been forgiven, so she has shown me much love. But a person who is forgiven little shows only little love."

Then Jesus said to the woman, "Your sins are forgiven."

The men at the table said among themselves, "Who is this man, that he goes around forgiving sins?"

And Jesus said to the woman, "Your faith has saved you; go in peace."

(Luke 7:44–50)

Simon, the host and Pharisee/rule-keeper, had neglected to honor his guest, Jesus, according to the cultural norms and customs of the time. The sinful woman, however, had bucked those same customs, yet somehow managed to honor Jesus in an even more intimate and meaningful way. Jesus flipped the table at that meal. He turned from the host and looked into the eyes of this woman with her hair falling around her, all of which was counter-cultural as well, and determined she—this outcast—was worthy of His attention and forgiveness. Jesus preferred the unclean woman over the proper host, the shameful sinner over the self-righteous Pharisee, and the scandalous, emotional wreck of a woman over the civilized man.

And he gives grace generously. As the scriptures say, "God opposes the proud but gives grace to the humble."

(James 4:6)

Jesus goes beyond forgiveness to reinstate our blamelessness, to lift us from shame and misunderstanding, and to restore our righteousness and our reputations . . . just like He did for this ostracized woman. Now, that's what I call some table-flippin'.

Jesus is not okay with any of us being sidelined or confined to the outskirts. Injustice, discrimination, and oppression hold no place in our Savior's kingdom of love, mercy, and compassion. Not only does He see us, but He welcomes, forgives, and offers us peace. Jesus lifts us out of our shame, flips the tables of inequity, and restores the right order in our lives and situations. For a person feeling misunderstood or accused, it is a priceless gift.

> *Jesus lifts us out of our shame, flips the tables of inequity, and restores the right order in our lives and situations.*

We've heard the phrase, "Don't sit at tables Jesus has already flipped over." I say, take it a step further: let's flip some tables ourselves, shatter the norms, include the marginalized, and drive out inequity . . . just like Jesus.

Live like Jesus

Inside . . .

Do you have tables in your life that Jesus wants to flip over? Do your words or actions increase the marginalization of others, or do they invite, forgive, and restore?

. . . and Out

Look for those on the outskirts of society. These are the people Jesus went after with all His heart. Start with a cause close to your heart, because He put it on your heart for a reason. Find a way to get involved and help flip the tables of injustice.

Jesus with Skin On

—— Serve like Jesus ——

This morning started predictably for me: praying in the shower. Knowing I'd carved time out of my schedule today to write a laity devotional, I specifically prayed, "God, clear out my ideas of what I should write about, and instead, tell me what You want to say."

I finished showering and began getting ready when I heard the unmistakable, high-pitched whirr of a Weed Eater. Assuming it was one of my neighbors, I continued with my morning tasks. Then, I remembered how my sweet dad had shown up at our house unannounced just days before and started weed-eating the large expanse of property outside our fence. Sometimes, he does amazing, servant-minded things just like this, even though he's in his late seventies, and even though I have both an able-bodied man in his forties and a teenage boy living in this house.

Sure enough, I peeked out the window and saw my daddy hard at work. I sent my son out to greet his grandfather and to ask for a lesson in how to safely operate a Weed Eater, so the younger could take over for the older. I watched through the window as my dad offered a lesson to his grandson, and then allowed the teen to take responsibility for the work. My dad stood at a distance, protectively watching his grandson's every move. When the Weed-Eater stopped working, they went to the truck bed together and repaired it to proper working order, and then the job continued.

Words cannot describe what it means to me to have a father who not only believes in Jesus but also strives to emulate Him every day. I didn't ask my dad to do yard work at my house; he just showed up, tools at the ready. I didn't ask my dad to instruct my son on how to weed eat; he just patiently started to teach him. I didn't ask my dad to stay a while longer to ensure my son didn't get hurt or encounter a problem with this new task; he just continued to watch over him. I didn't ask my dad to greet my daughter with a bear hug when she arrived on the scene; he just smiled broadly and stretched out his arms as soon as he saw her.

My dad looks like Jesus with skin on to me. He doesn't serve others—and especially his family—for attention or praise. He serves because he wants to love like Jesus and because he is immensely grateful for what God has done in his life. I think God wants us, His church, to look this way, too. Let's revisit Jesus washing His disciples' feet to see how He modeled this kind of servitude.

> When he had finished washing their feet, he put on his clothes and returned to his place. "Do you understand what I have done for you?" he asked them. "You call me 'Teacher' and 'Lord,' and rightly so, for that is what I am. Now that I, your Lord and Teacher, have washed your feet, you also should wash one another's feet. I have set you an example that you should do as I have done for you. Very truly I tell you, no servant is greater than his master, nor is a messenger greater than the one who sent him. Now that you know these things, you will be blessed if you do them."
>
> (John 13:12–17 NIV)

Christ was talking about a great deal more than physical foot washing. Foot washing was an act performed by a servant in the household—the lowest of the servants. Jesus wanted to emphasize that not only was He willing to perform acts of service for His friends, but He was willing to lower Himself to the rank of a slave. He knew it was a short matter of time before He would be asked to give up His life for these same friends, and all of mankind. Jesus's ultimate act of service was giving up His physical life so we might gain eternal life. He instructed the disciples to live as He did.

> "This is my commandment: Love each other in the same way I have loved you. There is no greater love than to lay down one's life for one's friends."
>
> (John 15:12–13)

When it comes to serving others, we want to bring the kingdom of God down to earth. We want to love others the way God has loved us. Nowhere in His kingdom do we find room for egos, comparison, selfishness, or conceit. As Pastor Lukas Lezon of Lifebridge Church said, "It's hard to throw stones if you're busy washing feet."[15] We should be looking at the world with an eye for where people are hurting, and go and serve there.

I read a post on Instagram that summed up these ideas well. It said, "How safe are the vulnerable among us? How loved do the unlovable feel? How much do we give to the ones who can't give back? How loud do we get when the oppressed are being silenced? Is there food for the hungry? Space for the immigrant? These are the questions that matter."[16]

Jesus expressed similar sentiments while teaching about the final judgment.

> "'For I was hungry, and you fed me. I was thirsty, and

you gave me a drink. I was a stranger, and you invited me into your home. I was naked, and you gave me clothing. I was sick, and you cared for me. I was in prison, and you visited me.'

Then these righteous ones will reply, 'Lord, when did we ever see you hungry and feed you? Or thirsty and give you something to drink? Or a stranger and show you hospitality? Or naked and give you clothing? When did we ever see you sick or in prison and visit you?'

And the King will say, 'I tell you the truth, when you did it to one of the least of these my brothers and sisters, you were doing it to me!'"

(Matthew 25:35–40)

Jesus didn't just serve people who looked like Him, lived near Him, believed like Him, and worshiped like Him. He helped men, women, children, sinners, Israelites, Samaritans, gentiles, servants, the diseased, outcasts, and more. Jesus came for the poor, the captive, and the broken-hearted (see Isaiah 61:1–2). In other words, He came for the marginalized.

In Matthew, chapter 15, we learn of a time during Jesus's ministry when He spent three straight days ministering and healing people near the Sea of Galilee. As the third day drew to a close, Jesus realized the people were unwilling to leave Him to find food.

Then Jesus called his disciples and told them, "I feel sorry for these people. They have been here with me for three days, and they have nothing left to eat. I don't want to send them away hungry, or they will faint along the way."

(Matthew 15:32)

In response, Jesus performed a miracle. He took a tiny portion of food, prayed over it, and gave it to the disciples to serve the crowd. In the end, Jesus fed 4,000 men, plus women and children. He and the disciples served the crowd a meal, despite their exhaustion. This shows us Jesus isn't only interested in meeting our spiritual concerns, but our physical ones as well. Serving like Jesus means meeting others' most basic and dire human needs, even when that means going beyond our comfort zones.

To cultivate a servant's mindset, we must shift our focus to promoting and elevating others, not ourselves. We spend the majority of our time and energy, though, striving to be the best in our fields; in fact, we spend the majority of our lives doing this, all while claiming we are doing it "for the glory of God." But do our efforts even matter to Him? I believe the extent to which Jesus cares that we are excellent in our chosen careers is proportionate only to the extent to which we use those careers to serve Him and serve others. If we get this wrong, we have missed the mark entirely.

> *Serving like Jesus means meeting others' most basic and dire human needs, even when that means going beyond our comfort zones.*

At the end of our lives, what is it we want to hear from our Heavenly Father? Is it, "Well done, my good and faithful banker? Teacher? Writer? Lawyer?" I know I want to hear, "Well done, my good and faithful *servant*!"

If we want to live like Jesus, we need to empty ourselves of our self-righteousness, comfort, and security, and serve others the way He did. Oftentimes, if we want to be "Jesus with skin on," all we need to do is simply show up for those in need, accompanied by a willing heart and whatever tools or food we've already been given. It's not as difficult to serve others as we often think. We need only look to Jesus's example and follow Him.

LIVE LIKE JESUS

Inside ...

We cannot say we are Christians and refuse to serve others. We cannot claim we love Jesus if we fail to love and help His people. We are not all called to be missionaries to remote parts of the world, but we are called to do *something*. Your mission field may be your home, your neighborhood, the school at the end of your block, and more. Ask God where He wants you to help and serve. He will answer because far too many of His people are suffering and in need.

. . . and Out

You can do it. That thing God told you above? That's the one. With God's help, you can do it. Don't hesitate, and don't make excuses. Just take the first step. God will be with you. Go.

Dead and Unexpected Places

—— *Bring Life like Jesus* ——

I slipped off my flip-flops and walked across the cool, green grass of the backyard, tossing giant burr oak acorns over the back fence as I made my way to the garden. An arborist once told me I could plant oak trees this way, thanks to the deer herds on the back property. I can only hope.

I opened the gate to the garden and breathed deeply at the sights and smells of my little slice of heaven-on-earth: a rainbow of zinnias, fragrant sweet basil, ripening tomatoes, and leafy green lettuce. It's not that unusual, I know, except for one thing: it's December. Inside, my house is decorated for Christmas, but my garden looks like it's early summer!

Months ago, during one of the worst droughts the Texas Hill Country has ever seen, I gave up on all these plants. Water restrictions forbade their nourishment, so I sadly left them to wilt and burn in the scorching summer sun. I didn't have the energy in those record-breaking-heat days to pull the mostly dead plants, so I just left them alone. Finally, in early fall, rain fell once again. Surprisingly, signs of life emerged from my little garden. Two months later, and everywhere I look I can see full blooms and ripening vegetables. Even in the pea gravel between the garden's beds, colorful zinnias peek out and blossom. It reminds me of the end of chapter 61 in

Isaiah, which says, "His righteousness will be like a garden in early spring, with plants springing up everywhere."

In dead and unexpected circumstances, God brings forth life. Jesus had a knack for doing this exact thing with *people*. In three different cases, Scripture tells us Jesus brought dead people back to life. We already learned about Lazarus from the *Grieve like Jesus* chapters, so let's take a look at the other two examples.

In dead and unexpected circumstances, God brings forth life.

Jairus, a leader in the synagogue, sought out Jesus so he could ask Him to heal his profoundly ill daughter. Before they reached Jairus's home, Jairus received word his daughter had died. When Jesus heard what had happened, He said to Jairus, "Don't be afraid. Just have faith, and she will be healed" (Luke 8:50). They continued traveling until they reached Jairus's home.

> The house was filled with people weeping and wailing, but he said, "Stop the weeping! She isn't dead; she's only asleep."
>
> But the crowd laughed at him because they all knew she had died. Then Jesus took her by the hand and said in a loud voice, "My child, get up!"
>
> And at that moment her life returned, and she immediately stood up! Then Jesus told them to give her something to eat.
>
> (Luke 8:52–55)

First, Jesus calmed Jairus's fear. Next, He encouraged Jairus to have faith. Then, He comforted Jairus by promising to heal his daughter. Finally, Jesus kept His word to Jairus and brought the girl back to life the instant He took her hand. Jesus brought emotional, spiritual, and physical life to this family, all in one encounter.

A similar miracle occurs in the story of the widow from the village of Nain.

> Soon afterward Jesus went with his disciples to the village of Nain, and a large crowd followed him. A funeral procession was coming out as he approached the village gate. The young man who had died was a widow's only son, and a large crowd from the village was with her. When the Lord saw her, his heart overflowed with compassion.
>
> "Don't cry!" he said. Then he walked over to the coffin and touched it, and the bearers stopped. "Young man," he said, "I tell you, get up." Then the dead boy sat up and began to talk! And Jesus gave him back to his mother.
>
> (Luke 7:11–15)

When Jesus saw this widow mourning her only son, He was filled with empathy and moved to action. Again, we see Jesus offering compassion, this time when He tells the widow not to cry. Christ then brought the dead son back to life, much like God would do later for His Son.

In these moments when Jesus literally and physically returned life to the dead, we see Him enter into people's suffering with kindness and mercy. We may not be able to raise a person from the dead and impart life again, but we can certainly model Jesus's brand of life-giving compassion. In addition, we can take a look at occasions where Christ offered invitations to spiritual life and abundant life, and we can aim to do the same.

The apostle John recounts a parable Jesus told about thieves, sheep, a shepherd, and a gate. In this story, a gatekeeper opens the gate for the sheep, calls them by name, gathers the flock, and then walks ahead of the flock with the sheep following him. Those listening to the parable were confused by it.

> Those who heard Jesus use this illustration didn't understand what he meant, so he explained it to them: "I tell you the truth, I am the gate for the sheep. All who came before me were thieves and robbers. But the true sheep did not listen to them. Yes, I am the gate. Those who come in through me will be saved. They will come and go freely and will find good pastures. The thief's purpose is to steal and kill and destroy. My purpose is to give them a rich and satisfying life."
>
> (John 10:6–10)

We often hear this parable used to explain Jesus as the only entryway to heaven. Although this is correct, for this chapter, I'd like to focus on what Jesus says about the sheep. Jesus says those entering through the gate receive salvation, but also the freedom to "come and go freely and find good pastures." Jesus is not only offering salvation; He is offering freedom and redemption. He goes on to say His "purpose is to give them a rich and satisfying life." Jesus does not rubber-stamp our foreheads with the word *Saved* and leave us to our own ends. No, Christ's invitation goes beyond the moment of rescue and offers abundant life.

We know from the chapters on grieving that Jesus brought His friend, Lazarus, back from the dead. But if we look at the passages surrounding this miraculous encounter, we see Jesus also offered life to Lazarus's sister, Martha, who went out to meet Jesus as He approached her village.

Jesus told her, "Your brother will rise again."

"Yes," Martha said, "he will rise when everyone else rises, at the last day."

Jesus told her, "I am the resurrection and the life. Anyone who believes in me will live, even after dying. Everyone who lives in me and believes in me will never ever die. Do you believe this, Martha?"

(John 11:23–26)

Jesus was less concerned with Lazarus's physical death than He was with the spiritual deaths of His friends. Remember, Jesus came so they might have life and have it abundantly. Here we see Jesus teaching Martha that He is the resurrection and the life; in other words, He is the only way to spiritual resurrection after death—*eternal* life—and also the only way to experience meaningful life on earth. Recognize the important question Jesus asks Martha after He explains these things to her. He asks, "Do you believe this, Martha?" All of us must answer this same question for ourselves, before the Son of God.

> *When we bring Jesus into our everyday situations, relationships, and conversations, new life erupts.*

So, how can we bring life into dead places? After all, we're not divine like Jesus.

And this is what God has testified: He has given us eternal life, and this life is in his Son. Whoever has the

177

Son has life; whoever does not have God's Son does not have life.

(1 John 5:11–12)

According to this verse, Jesus is the key. He holds life. He *is* life itself. He offers both abundant life and eternal life, freely, to all who believe in Him. When we bring Jesus into our everyday situations, relationships, and conversations, new life erupts. Living like Jesus creates an opportunity for relationships wherein the Holy Spirit can prompt others to change and seek God. We can't accomplish this on our own, but when we try to live more like Jesus and we offer the Good News to others, life springs forth. It helps to focus more on our spiritual lives than our temporal ones. And then, just like me eyeing my garden, we can all watch life springing forth from dead and unexpected places.

LIVE LIKE JESUS

Inside...

Have you entrusted the care of your life to the giver of life, Jesus Christ? Why or why not? Have you entrusted Him with your eternal life?

...and Out

It's easy to look around the world and see death and decay, but when we bring Jesus into the equation, everything changes. Look for new ways and opportunities to speak life to everyone you come in contact with, and to constantly point others to the path of life everlasting.

Jesus, in his Heart . . . and in his Tummy

—— Pray like Jesus, part 1 ——

I distinctly remember the morning my four-year-old son asked me some surprisingly deep questions about faith and salvation. Like many kids, he'd always attended children's Sunday school and church, and he learned the Lord's Prayer in pre-school. He arrived at this young age with some truly mature spiritual decisions, though.

"Mommy," he began, "I want to ask Jesus to come live inside my heart."

"That is the most important choice you will ever make, Sweetie," I replied. "Can you tell me what you think that means?"

Johnathan replied, "It means I love Jesus, and Jesus forgives me, and then I can live with Him in heaven forever."

"That's exactly right," I said.

But Johnathan interrupted, saying, "But *how* does He get into my heart, Mommy? Do you have to cut a hole in my tummy?"

Oh, good gracious! Johnathan was deeply relieved to find out we didn't need to take a scalpel to his little abdomen to make an entryway for Jesus, but knowing he was willing to make such a sacrifice impressed upon me just how serious he was about this decision. After additional explanations and reassurances, my son said a prayer of salvation that morning, right there at our kitchen table.

Thankfully for us all, prayer comprises the gateway for Jesus to grant our salvation, as well as all the other blessings God has in store for us. Even Jesus—both human and divine—spent a great deal of time in prayer, according to the Gospels. Based on this, we can surmise that prayer should constitute a critical part of our lives as people of faith. Jesus confirmed this by telling us *how* God wants us to pray.

> "When you pray, don't be like the hypocrites who love to pray publicly on street corners and in the synagogues where everyone can see them. I tell you the truth, that is all the reward they will ever get. But when you pray, go away by yourself, shut the door behind you, and pray to your Father in private. Then your Father, who sees everything, will reward you.
>
> "When you pray, don't babble on and on as the Gentiles do. They think their prayers are answered merely by repeating their words again and again. Don't be like them, for your Father knows exactly what you need even before you ask him!"

(Matthew 6:5–8)

According to Jesus, we are to pray privately, to God alone, without pretense, and with faith that God already knows what we need before we even ask. But, just in case we humans can't fully grasp those ideas, Jesus went a step further and told us exactly what words to use when praying. We refer to those words as the Lord's Prayer, and we find them in Matthew 6, verses 9–13.

We often say the Lord's Prayer during church services (as groups) and by memory. Both of these practices make it easy for us to perform rote recitation of this prayer, rather than thinking critically about the words we are saying to the Lord. If Jesus instructed us to say these specific words, they must carry power and meaning for us. Let's break down Jesus's prayer phrase by phrase.

Our Father . . . This reminds us of our inclusion in the community of faith, bringing to mind that the God of Adam and Eve, Noah, Moses, Abraham, David, and Jesus is the same God we worship today. This God is also a loving father, and we can come to Him like the needy children we are—with our hurts and fears, as well as our adoration.

who art in heaven . . . Who sits on the great throne? God Almighty does. He is sovereign over all creation.

> *If Jesus instructed us to say these specific words, they must carry power and meaning for us.*

hallowed be Thy name . . . The very name of God, like Yahweh Himself, is completely holy. Because of this, we strive for holiness in our lives as well, to bring glory to Him.

Thy kingdom come . . . We ask for Jesus to return to earth in final glory and victory and for the kingdom of God to be established here forever. This also reminds us to bring a little heaven down to earth while we're here, by focusing on His kingdom work in and around our lives.

Thy will be done on earth as it is in heaven . . . May God's will for us and the world around us take precedence over any other thing happening. May nothing thwart the perfect will of God. Furthermore, may we be sensitive to the leading of God in our own lives so we may help in bringing about His will here on the earth. "Thy will be done" forms our emphatic, in-advance "Yes!" to all God may ask of us.

Give us this day our daily bread . . . Remember the manna God provided Moses and the Israelites in the desert? Every day God gave them just enough for that day, so they would learn to trust and rely on Him alone. This should be our prayer: God, please give me just enough, every day, that I may continue serving you. The "our" in this passage reminds us we are privileged to pray for others' needs, as well as our own. "Daily bread" goes beyond just our physical needs and includes our emotional and spiritual needs as well. The Lord provides what we need to continue serving Him.

and forgive us our trespasses . . . Some versions use the word *debts* here. The balance scales are off because Jesus paid the cost of our sins for us. Forgive us for our many past sins, God. Only Jesus can save us.

as we forgive those who trespass against us . . . What is our response to God's forgiveness? We forgive others, right now, in this present moment. All of them for every reason. Why? Because that's what we just finished asking God to do for us.

And lead us not into temptation . . . We see situations in the Bible (Job, for example, and Jesus in the desert) when God *allowed* temptation to occur. In our weakness, we ask for a different fate. We ask for God's strength and protection for us and those we love, now and in the future.

but deliver us from the enemy . . . Only God can protect us from the schemes of the enemy, and He will claim ultimate victory over evil. We pray for mercy, salvation, and deliverance.

for Thine is the kingdom, and the power, and the glory forever . . . God is the Alpha and Omega. Everything is His and His alone, now and forever. God wins. He deserves all our praise.

Amen. Make it so, Lord. Make it so.

When our emotions and thoughts overwhelm us to the point of not knowing how or what to pray, we can always turn to the

Lord's Prayer. Say it over and over again, if that is all that comes to mind. Just know that even when words do not come, God knows and somehow still hears us.

> And the Holy Spirit helps us in our weakness. For example, we don't know what God wants us to pray for. But the Holy Spirit prays for us with groanings that cannot be expressed in words. And the Father who knows all hearts knows what the Spirit is saying, for the Spirit pleads for us believers in harmony with God's own will.
>
> (Romans 8:26–27)

We boast a mighty Father in heaven, and He is on our side. We don't have to cut open our tummies to know and be known by Him; all we need to do is engage in a simple, honest conversation with Him. How loved and understood are we, because Jesus already gave us the words.

Live like Jesus

Inside . . .

Have you ever really stopped to consider the meaning of the words in the Lord's Prayer before now? Take time to do this if you haven't already. Meditate on the words Jesus gave us.

. . . and Out

We don't serve a quiet, distant God, but one who listens to us and speaks to us in return. Thank Him for the blessing and gift He has given us to come directly to Him in prayer. Say the Lord's Prayer today, slowly, and let the intimacy with your Heavenly Father wash over you.

I Want It All!

—— *Pray like Jesus, part 2* ——

Johnathan, eyeing his sister Rachel's last two crackers, asked, "Wachel, can I have bofe of those?"

Rachel responded, "No, but you can have one of them."

Johnathan whined, "I want bofe!!"

Rachel explained calmly and pragmatically, "Johnathan. You can have one or none."

Little brother answered, "Nooooo . . . it's one or two. And I want *two!!*"

I often wonder if this is how we sound praying to our Heavenly Father. How much of our time in prayer do we spend asking for things we want? Don't get me wrong; God wants to hear our pleas and petitions, but if this is the extent of our prayer life, we are missing out on a great deal of what God desires for us.

If we want a deep and meaningful prayer life, we should model the prayer life of Jesus. In the Gospels, we read of numerous times and circumstances in

> *If Jesus, the Son of God, prayed often, we probably should, too.*

which Jesus prayed: before raising Lazarus from the dead, at His baptism, before feeding the multitudes, after He withdrew from the crowds, before choosing the disciples, at the Last Supper, in the garden of Gethsemane before His arrest, at the transfiguration, during the Sermon on the Mount, before walking on water, and many other times. If Jesus, the Son of God, prayed often, we probably should, too.

As we discussed in the last chapter, Jesus taught us to pray using the specific words of the Lord's Prayer. However, Jesus instructs us further in His teaching about prayer in the verses that follow the Lord's Prayer. Jesus tells us to be *persistent* in our prayers—in our asking—because our Heavenly Father wants to give us good gifts.

> "And so I tell you, keep on asking, and you will receive what you ask for. Keep on seeking, and you will find. Keep on knocking, and the door will be opened to you. For everyone who asks, receives. Everyone who seeks, finds. And to everyone who knocks, the door will be opened."
>
> (Luke 11:9–10)

Is simple persistence enough? I don't think it's quite that simple, but the story Jesus tells here is likened to a stranger knocking on a door continuously until the homeowner finally gives in and answers. I mean, why *wouldn't* we try this approach? What do we have to lose?

Jesus told another parable emphasizing the importance of persisting in prayer. He described a widow who continued to appear before a corrupt judge, repeatedly requesting justice in a dispute.

> "The judge ignored her for a while, but finally he said to himself, 'I don't fear God or care about people, but this woman is driving me crazy. I'm going to see that she gets justice, because she is wearing me out with her constant requests!'"

Then the Lord said, "Learn a lesson from this unjust judge. Even he rendered a just decision in the end. So don't you think God will surely give justice to his chosen people who cry out to him day and night? Will he keep putting them off?"

(Luke 18:4–7)

Clearly, we need to pay attention to this idea of persisting in our prayers. In addition to persistence, according to Scripture, God also responds to our *passion* when praying.

While Jesus was here on earth, he offered prayers and pleadings, with a loud cry and tears, to the one who could rescue him from death. And God heard his prayers because of his deep reverence for God.

(Hebrews 5:7)

I find this passage highly interesting because it says Jesus prayed passionately to the God who could rescue Him from death and God heard His prayers. However, we know Jesus wasn't rescued from death, at least, not in the human way we think of death. The passage says Jesus's "deep reverence" and "loud cry and tears" moved His Heavenly Father to answer His prayers, though. This leaves us to understand that God answered, but maybe His answer wasn't the one Jesus wanted. And let's face it, friends, this is *Jesus* we're talking about here. If anyone held some sway over the Heavenly Father, it was His Son, Jesus! Based on this, though, we can rest assured God does hear and answer our prayers, especially when we offer them from a passionate, reverent heart. When we pray, God desires our honest and true feelings above all else, not just pretty words.

In addition to persistence and passion, another key to prayer involves listening and attentiveness. Specifically, we need to learn to hear what God is saying, rather than just talking our faces off in His direction. How much harder do we make it on ourselves when we want to hear from God, but we've already decided what we want Him to say? In other words, we listen to confirm our preconceived ideas, rather than to affirm God's wisdom and omniscience. We should enter into prayer ready to listen, expecting God to meet us there.

> *We should enter into prayer ready to listen, expecting God to meet us there.*

In my first book, *Grace-Faced*, I explain prayer is not a means-to-an-end, or an exercise in rubbing a magic lamp so the big genie in the sky will fulfill our wishes. Instead, prayer is about cultivating a relationship with God. I wrote, "We should pray, not until we feel God has heard us, but until we have heard God."[17] He wants to have a conversation with us, not so our situation will change, but so *we* will change.

Julian of Norwich, the Benedictine monk and arguably one of the first truly great female writers of the English language, speaks to the importance of praying at all times, regardless of feelings. In number 89 of 365 reasons to pray, she says, "Pray, even if you feel nothing, see nothing. For when you are dry, empty, sick, or weak, at such a time is your prayer most pleasing to God, even though you may find little joy in it. This is true of all believing prayer."[18]

So, how should our prayer life look? Persistent, passionate, attentive, and relational. It should also house variety, and not feel rote or boring. A rich, fulfilling prayer life consists of many kinds of prayer: meditative (clearing the mind to spiritually listen), contemplative (focusing deeply on a particular idea or passage), praise, supplication or intercession, thanksgiving, adoration, and confession. All are holy because God is there, a part of the conversation.

Pastor David Payne says, "Prayer is a gateway for the Holy Spirit to have more and more influence over our lives." In other words, praying brings us closer to God and allows Him to better work in and through us. And why do we pray, if not to know God better?

Maybe it's okay to enter prayer like my son entered the conversation with his sister, wanting it all . . . but only if the "all" we seek is a total revelation of the nature of our Heavenly Father and an intimate connection with Almighty God. His goal is always to draw us into an ever-deepening, loving relationship with Him.

> "For everyone who asks, receives. Everyone who seeks, finds. And to everyone who knocks, the door will be opened."
>
> (Matthew 7:8)

This day, choose to ask, seek, and knock. And, if you are moved to do so, storm the gates of heaven in prayer. Approach the throne passionately, persistently, attentively, and expectantly, knowing your requests reach your Father in heaven. And not just one or two of them, but all of them.

LIVE LIKE JESUS

Inside...

Think about your prayer life. Is it consistent, passionate, persistent, attentive, and relational? In which of these areas can you stand to improve? Consider finding a prayer partner so you can hold one another accountable for cultivating a rich and meaningful prayer life.

...and Out

Work out ways you can improve on that area of your prayer life that you listed above. And, if you've been praying for something for a very long time, don't give up! God wants you to pray without ceasing, and He honors our persistence.

White Whiskers and Other Reprehensible Things

—— Forgive like Jesus ——

One of my favorite Christmas morning moments happened the year our son, Johnathan, became fixated on ensuring Santa had milk, the very best of the Christmas cookies, and carrots for the reindeer on Christmas Eve. After setting up gifts and stockings while the children were sleeping, my husband, John, and I ate half the cookies, nibbled the carrots, and drank half the glass of milk in anticipation of Christmas morning.

When Johnathan came bounding into the living room the next morning before the break of dawn, he excitedly shouted, "Who wants to finish Santa's milk?!" To our surprise, he immediately backtracked, grimaced, and said, "Welllll . . . maybe no one. Santa probably left white whiskers in it."

Apparently, Santa's whiskers are a deal-breaker . . . a no-fly zone, even for the sleigh man. Johnathan couldn't tolerate even the thought of it.

As Christians, we feel this way about sin, don't we? Or, at least we believe we are *supposed* to feel this way about sin. We know some heinous, awful, deal-breaking sins occur out there in the world. I want us to ask ourselves this: Which sin is the most difficult to forgive? Which sin crosses a line we just can't abide by or "stomach"?

Which sin disqualifies the sinner from participating in the fullness of the kingdom of God, like serving as a leader or pastor, or enjoying the same fellowship with the rest of the church body? Do we have it in our minds? Now, let me ask this:

Why does *your* sin not disqualify *you* from those same blessings?

The answer is simple: it does. *All* sin separates us from communion with our holy and perfect Heavenly Father, so we *all* need forgiveness. We need Jesus to bridge this great divide for us. Jesus for you. Jesus for me. Jesus for everyone.

That's right, I said everyone. Even for "those people" . . . the people with *that* sin. The one that creeps us out. The one that makes us truly uncomfortable. The one with which we don't want to share a room, much less a pew. Maybe even the one that damaged us at some point beyond what we thought could be repaired. Whatever sin just came to mind, that's the one I am talking about. Yes, that one. Jesus died for *that* sin. He also died for *that* sinner. And all the other sins and sinners, too. In fact, Jesus just loved to share a meal and a conversation with *those* kinds of people. Those are the people He reached out to first. And He didn't just tolerate them for the sake of looking like a good Son of God. No, Jesus *befriended* them and even dared to ask them to *join Him in ministry to others*. That sin and those sinners we identified in our minds? Those are Jesus's kind of people. Those are the people Jesus went to great lengths to include and—dare I say—love. And, let's face it. Sometimes it's easier to die for someone than to live peacefully with them. Somehow, Jesus managed to succeed at both. Somehow, we usually manage to fail at both.

We're all familiar with the verse about not pointing out the sin in others. Jesus said:

> "Do not judge others, and you will not be judged. For
> you will be treated as you treat others. The standard
> you use in judging is the standard by which you will be
> judged. And why worry about a speck in your friend's
> eye when you have a log in your own? How can you
> think of saying to your friend, 'Let me help you get rid
> of that speck in your eye,' when you can't see past the
> log in your own eye?"
>
> (Matthew 7:1–4)

We need to concern ourselves with our own sins, rather than pointing out the sins in others. Jesus warns us that we will be judged by the same measure we use to judge others. If that's not the case for generosity, understanding, and forgiveness, then I don't know what is. Please, God, don't judge me in the same way I criticize others; teach me to forgive like Jesus!

In a time when it seems everyone wants to be known for what they are against rather than what they are for, I believe Jesus would drop down into the middle of our mess and do exactly what He did best the first time He walked this earth: love and forgive people. Not point fingers, but offer compassion. Not exclude, but welcome. He succinctly tells us:

Jesus warns us that we will be judged by the same measure we use to judge others.

> "Do not judge others, and you will not be judged. Do
> not condemn others, or it will all come back against you.
> Forgive others, and you will be forgiven."
>
> (Luke 6:37)

Jesus offered forgiveness countless times while He was here on earth. His particular brand of forgiveness was not flashy or demeaning, because Jesus also offered compassion and mercy when He offered forgiveness. I cherish the way Jesus drew near to the hurting, the accused, and the ashamed and offered them what they didn't even know they needed.

One of my favorite examples comes from the story of the paralytic.

> Some people brought to him a paralyzed man on a mat. Seeing their faith, Jesus said to the paralyzed man, "Be encouraged, my child! Your sins are forgiven."
>
> But some of the teachers of religious law said to themselves, "That's blasphemy! Does he think he's God?"
>
> Jesus knew what they were thinking, so he asked them, "Why do you have such evil thoughts in your hearts? Is it easier to say 'Your sins are forgiven,' or 'Stand up and walk'? So I will prove to you that the Son of Man has the authority on earth to forgive sins."
>
> Then Jesus turned to the paralyzed man and said, "Stand up, pick up your mat, and go home!"
>
> And the man jumped up and went home!
>
> (Matthew 9:2–7)

At this point in Jesus's ministry, people knew of His healing. This paralyzed man's friends brought him to Jesus for a paralysis cure, but Jesus knew what the man needed even more: forgiveness for his sins and reconciliation with God. So, Jesus offered the man forgiveness, but when the surrounding people balked at His pronouncement, Jesus chose to physically heal the man as well.

This encounter makes me wonder. Could it be our metaphorical hearts are even sicker than our bodies? Do our *spirits* need the Great Physician more than we realize? Is forgiveness the key to our healing and well-being? Jesus's actions seem to affirm these notions because He seemed to prioritize spiritual healing (through forgiveness) over physical healing.

And here's the kicker. We know Jesus came to heal the sinful rift between us and God and to offer Himself as atonement for all sin for all time. But the story doesn't end there. Jesus's gift of forgiveness was never meant to stay with us because God wants us to extend that same gift to the entire world. Remember "those" people? The forgiveness we have received, we are to offer them; and not just in death, but in life. Every day, we are to live like Jesus: not known by what we hate or whom we exclude, but by our love and forgiveness. So, the next time our sense of righteousness or spiritual pride causes us to look down our noses at others and vilify their sinful lives, remember we *all* sin and fall short, and it is Jesus who pays the price for us.

> *Jesus stands before a crowd of our accusers and fails to condemn or punish us; instead, He forgives us and takes our punishment on Himself.*

Think back one more time to the story in John, chapter 8, of the woman caught in adultery. Try to imagine how that woman felt— knowing her guilt and knowing the punishment for her crime—as she watched each man drop his stone and walk away, all because a man named Jesus stood up on her behalf. He has done the same for you and me. Jesus stands before a crowd of our accusers and fails to condemn or punish us; instead, He forgives us and takes our punishment on Himself.

Forgiving like Jesus doesn't mean overlooking others' sins. It means remembering we *all* sin, and it is *Jesus* who pays the price and bears the punishment for each one of us.

> Instead, be kind to each other, tenderhearted, forgiving one another, just as God through Christ has forgiven you.
>
> (Ephesians 4:32)

We all need the mercy and forgiveness of the Savior. And none of us needs Him any more than another. Well, except those of us who leave white whiskers in our milk . . . I mean, come on, that's just unforgivable.

Live like Jesus

Inside . . .

Do you find it difficult to forgive certain sins more than others? Why is this so? Does knowing all sins are equal in God's eyes—and that Jesus paid the same penalty for them all—change this thought pattern for you?

. . . and Out

Are you harboring unforgiveness for someone in your heart? If so, pray God will give you the desire and the strength to forgive that person. God can and will help you through this process, even when you don't want to do it.

A Little Less Talk and a Lot More Action

—— Listen and Speak like Jesus ——

The familiar strains of a sibling argument began to drift down the hallway and into the kitchen where I stood, preparing supper. I tuned in to the disagreement, ready to intervene if necessary, and overheard my four-year-old son exclaim, "Stop saying that so rudely to me every time I interrupt you!" I stopped mid-stir, not knowing quite how to respond to his angry statement. He was irate because his sister wouldn't allow him to keep interrupting her. I chuckled to myself and waited to see how his sister would respond.

As it turned out, little brother had hurt big sister's feelings, and while she tried to explain to him how she felt, he kept interjecting to make excuses, rather than listening to her. He wasn't apologizing but was explaining himself, and he didn't want to listen to how his actions had affected his sister. I know my son well enough to know his actions were based on love; he doesn't like to hurt others, and it pains him to hear how he has done so. By interrupting, he was trying to avoid confronting the knowledge he had hurt her. I think many of us do the same thing.

Listening and speaking, as the two often go hand-in-hand, prove difficult for children and adults alike. Just yesterday, a friend on social media truly, deeply hurt my feelings. I don't think she meant to hurt me. In fact, I don't think she even knew she'd hurt me, because I didn't respond in any way to her hurtful post. All she did was forward a post someone else had written. She probably even had good intentions for doing it, but it angered and wounded me.

Why didn't I respond? I reminded myself of Socrates's three-filter test before speaking. Was what I wanted to say true—and not just my version of truth, but universally true? Was what I wanted to say inherently good or kind? Was what I wanted to say useful?[19] When faced with these questions, I reminded myself that, yes, I have the *right* to say whatever I want, but I also know God will hold me accountable for my words. How my words affect others matters to God, so it should also matter to me.

I don't know if we give enough thought to the effect of our words before we let them fly into the universe, especially in the age of social media and instant, eternal publication. Intentions be damned, because all that truly matters is how we make others *feel*, because we are responsible for that. We need to use extreme caution and care when speaking to others, and most especially when speaking about sin in others, because I don't think any of us want that spotlight shined on all the hidden and not-so-hidden parts of our own lives that are less than glorifying to God. That's the thing about blanket, judgmental statements—we come off looking like ridiculous hypocrites because, as Romans 3:23 states, "everyone has sinned; we all fall short of God's glorious standard."

> **How do we speak of God's love and forgiveness in a way that invites others into fellowship, rather than excluding them from it?**

So, how do we go about sharing the truth of the Gospel without stepping on others' toes? How do we speak of God's love and for-giveness in a way that invites others into fellowship, rather than excluding them from it? How do we listen and speak like Jesus? Let's take a look at what Scripture tells us.

> Instead, we will speak the truth in love, growing in every way more and more like Christ, who is the head of his body, the church.
>
> (Ephesians 4:15)

We often hear in today's society about others "speaking their truth." We also hear, as Christians, how we should be speaking *the* truth. There is nothing inherently wrong with either; however, I believe it's important to listen to others' viewpoints and stories. We need to learn from one another if we want to be capable of sympathizing with and helping others. We all share this need to be heard. Couching our judgment of others' sins within the context of "speaking the truth" has inherent pitfalls. For one, none of us stands sinless, so what business do we have pointing out the sin in another? Second, it's difficult for a person to hear anything but condemna-tion when we arrive on the scene with our "sin police" sirens wailing, flashing our "good Christian" badges, and shouting Scripture into our megaphones. Condemnation is the exact opposite of Christ's approach to His message of truth! If we want to extend an invita-tion to the way of salvation, preaching damnation is probably the last place we should start.

Notice in so many of the personal interactions Jesus had with others, including the ones we've learned about up until this point, that He started by asking questions and then listening. When the storm arose, He asked the disciples why they were afraid. When He encountered the woman at the well, He asked about her personal life. After saving the woman caught in adultery from stoning, He asked where her accusers had gone. Jesus knew the answers to these questions, but He also knew conversation—especially the kind that leads to relationship, which was always His goal—is a two-way street that involves both listening and speaking. And, listening comes first.

We can also note in these same examples from Jesus's life that after He listened, He spoke to these people with words, tone, and a demeanor that exuded kindness and compassion. Even in situations where Jesus instructed His listeners to refrain from sin, He did so after first inviting them into His love and forgiveness and abundant and eternal life. In the words of Mister Rogers, "There's a world of difference between insisting on someone's doing something and estab-lishing an atmosphere in which that person can grow into wanting to do it."[20] Jesus seemed a master at this approach.

> *If we can learn to recognize Jesus in one another, we will automatically listen and speak with more kindness and compassion.*

Paul explains, in His letter to Colossae, how our speech should sound.

> But now is the time to get rid of anger, rage, malicious behavior, slander, and dirty language. Don't lie to each other, for you have stripped off your old sinful nature and all its wicked deeds. Put on your new nature, and be renewed as you learn to know your Creator and become like him.
>
> (Colossians 3:8–10)

Slander, dirty language, angry words, and lies all run contrary to Christ within us. Our mouths should take no part in such things. If you're anything like me, this proves a difficult task. But, the second part of this verse holds the answer we seek: we can enjoy new life and a new spirit while we're learning about God, and while we're in this process of becoming more like Jesus. That's extraordinarily good news, friends. Even while we are learning, we are growing more Christlike.

Later in Colossians, Paul again addresses how we should speak. He says our speech should be so full of grace that it entices others . . . no, not others, but *everyone*. Some of us may recognize this as the "words seasoned with salt" verse, although the New Living Translation below words it differently.

> Live wisely among those who are not believers, and make the most of every opportunity. Let your conversation be gracious and attractive so that you will have the right response for everyone.
>
> (Colossians 4:5–6)

If it's too difficult to imagine how Jesus would converse (as in, listen and speak) with a person in our given situation, maybe we could instead imagine ourselves conversing with Christ Himself. After all, He lives within each of us. If we can learn to recognize Jesus in one another, we will automatically listen and speak with more kindness and compassion. Maybe, in this case, we can strive to not only live like Jesus, but to converse as if Christ were sitting directly across from us.

LIVE LIKE JESUS

Inside...

Which is more difficult for you: listening like Jesus or speaking like Jesus? Neither involves condemnation, and both require patience and kindness. If listening or conversing like Jesus comes naturally to you, how could you maximize this gift to bring others to Christ?

...and Out

The next time you face a difficult or contentious conversation, picture Jesus sitting across from you. Remember to listen for understanding rather than just planning your next response. Do not try to outwit your counterpart, but instead focus on cultivating a relationship. In fact, in all our conversations, we should be striving to build relationships. What changes can you make to your conversational habits and patterns with this relationship-building in mind?

Where's My Super Suit?

—— *Rescue like Jesus* ——

"Dad," said the shaky voice on the other end of the phone line, "I hit a car. I'm okay, but I don't know what to do."

All three of my children caused fender benders within the first few months of getting their driver's licenses. Thankfully, all three were minor and happened here in our hometown while they still lived under our roof, making it easier for us to help them through the ordeals. I noticed all three of my kids, following their accidents, did the same thing first: they called their dad. Now, many people may think they called their dad because he knows a lot about cars and would therefore be of more assistance, but that's not the case. No, our kids reached out to their father because they knew he would drop everything and rush to help them, and in doing so, would take control of the situation and make them feel safe again.

My husband paints a beautiful picture of our Heavenly Father for our kids. They didn't worry their dad would get angry or act unfairly, harshly, or abusively in the face of their mistakes. We should all be blessed with a dad like this—a father we can truly count on. In truth, we all share that in our Heavenly Father. We don't claim just *any* daddy, but as Christians, we can boast in the same, all-powerful, Creator-of-all-things, proverbial super-suit-wearing dad. Oftentimes, when we're in big trouble, we go straight to Daddy—the big guy upstairs. We know we can count on Him to race to our aid, calm our fears, and take control. The apostle Paul cites a similar faith in his second letter to the Corinthians.

> In fact, we expected to die. But as a result, we stopped relying on ourselves and learned to rely only on God, who raises the dead. And he did rescue us from mortal danger, and he will rescue us again. We have placed our confidence in him, and he will continue to rescue us.
>
> (2 Corinthians 1:9–10)

One reason we have this faith that God will rescue us is because Jesus modeled this behavior when He was here on earth. Time and again, Jesus not only offered His help to those in need, but He offered total rescue.

Peter, for example, cried out to Jesus to save him as he walked towards Him on the water.

> Then Peter called to him, "Lord, if it's really you, tell me to come to you, walking on the water."
>
> "Yes, come," Jesus said. So Peter went over the side of the boat and walked on the water toward Jesus. But when he saw the strong wind and the waves, he was terrified and began to sink.
>
> "Save me, Lord!" he shouted. Jesus immediately reached out and grabbed him.
>
> "You have so little faith," Jesus said. "Why did you doubt me?"
>
> (Matthew 14:28–31)

The word "immediately" in the verse brings me great comfort. Peter cried out for help and Jesus *immediately* reached out and saved him. Jesus didn't call back, "Paddle harder!" or "Keep going! You can do it!" His response was like that of a sympathetic father, immediately moved by the panic in his child's voice to do anything necessary to bring his child relief.

Jesus performed countless rescues while here on earth, everything from physical disease, persecution, death, eternal damnation, and demonic possession. In all these cases, these people—like Peter in the story above—knew they could not save themselves. In desperation, fear, and torment, they cried out to the only One capable of saving them.

> *Time and again, Jesus not only offered His help to those in need, but He offered total rescue.*

One such man was named Legion. He desperately needed rescue, for he was tormented by numerous evil spirits living inside of him. The Gospel of Matthew says Legion often escaped the shackles and chains meant to confine him and wandered the hills howling and cutting himself with sharp stones.

> When Jesus was still some distance away, the man saw him, ran to meet him, and bowed low before him. With a shriek, he screamed, "Why are you interfering with me, Jesus, Son of the Most High God? In the name of God, I beg you, don't torture me!"
>
> For Jesus had already said to the spirit, "Come out of the man, you evil spirit." Then Jesus demanded, "What is your name?"

And he replied, "My name is Legion, because there are many of us inside this man."

Then the evil spirits begged him again and again not to send them to some distant place. There happened to be a large herd of pigs feeding on the hillside nearby. "Send us into those pigs," the spirits begged. "Let us enter them."

So Jesus gave them permission. The evil spirits came out of the man and entered the pigs, and the entire herd of about 2,000 pigs plunged down the steep hillside into the lake and drowned in the water.

(Mark 5:6–13)

I find comfort in Legion's rescue as well, knowing even evil minions must bow down to the authority of the Son of God. They preferred living inside a herd of pigs and plummeting to their death to Jesus sending them back to hell. It's amazing to realize we have uninhibited access to the very same rescuer as Legion.

Note I used the word "uninhibited." When we look at the rescues Jesus performed, none of these people did anything to "earn" his or her deliverance. The truth is, none of us deserves rescue. We can't earn it, meaning no one can place stipulations on it, either.

Oh, how easily we forget this. Our natural desire for equality often leads us to impose conditions on rescuing others. We want others to justify their circumstances before we will come to their aid. We create exceptions to our willingness to help. We ask questions like: Have they exhausted all other means of helping themselves before coming to us for help? Have they proven their loyalty to the church with their offerings, attendance, and service? Are they believers? Have they followed all our nation's laws, upheld all the cultural norms and traditions, and paid all their debts? Have they even *asked* for help? If people could "earn our rescue," they likely wouldn't need our help in the first place.

Remember the story I discussed in the *Forgive like Jesus* chapter, about the men who brought a paralyzed friend to Jesus for healing? In that story, we see Jesus rescue a person who not only didn't "earn" it but who didn't even *ask* for it! The Bible credits this man's *friends* with Jesus's forgiving and healing response to him.

As we can see, sometimes even the faith of a person's friends can place him or her directly in the path of Jesus's heroics. That means we can carry people to Jesus in prayer, too. We can stop and help those in need. We can point others to our Savior, Jesus Christ. Jesus didn't ask for people's qualifications or for them to "state their case" for rescue. He simply saw suffering and moved to eradicate it. He offered generous amounts of grace and mercy and an invitation to abundant life free from sin and shame. We can, and should, do the same.

> *Jesus didn't ask for people's qualifications or for them to "state their case" for rescue. He simply saw suffering and moved to eradicate it.*

If we want to live like Jesus, we need to rescue those around us. We should want to be others' first call when life takes ugly, unexpected turns. We should want to be the kind of person others know they can count on for help and safety. We should model trustworthiness and faithfulness, just like Jesus. And just like Superman (and my husband), we should answer those panicked phone calls, put on our "super suits," and set off on another rescuing adventure.

Live like Jesus

Inside . . .

Have you ever considered your attitude towards those you help? Do you only offer help to those you deem worthy of assistance? Do you expect some sort of payment in return? Does your rescue, unlike Jesus's brand of total rescue, come with conditions?

. . . and Out

So many people around us need rescue from a variety of physical, mental, emotional, and spiritual issues. Carry these people to Jesus in prayer, and if He gives you specific instructions, follow through and act on them. Remember your own need for rescue and in response offer the gift of Jesus's salvation to everyone you meet.

Buried or Burned

—— Die like Jesus ——

"Mommy, when you're dead, do you wanna' be buried or get burned?" Johnathan asked.

Stumped by my young son's question about grown-up funeral decisions, I stumbled momentarily while trying to figure out how he even knew about such things. At this point, we passed the golf course and he said, "I want to play golf again. But not right now, because there's ducks out there. Oh! Cooper is getting more chickens!"

With my mind spinning from the rapid-fire, random information coming at me courtesy of my preschooler, I resorted to simply shaking my head and muttering "uh-huh" in his general direction.

Why on earth was this kid thinking about burial and cremation? Death isn't exactly a topic most of us want to discuss, and yet, death is the one thing in our future we all hold in common. Even Jesus, in His limited time here, faced death. The question remains: how do we handle it? As always, our best guide goes by the name of Jesus.

As the time for Jesus to be crucified drew near, He chose to celebrate the religious ceremony called Passover with His closest friends. He did not abandon tradition, but instead used the opportunity to teach the disciples about the fulfillment of prophecy unfolding before them in the coming hours. He also chose to model servant leadership by washing the disciples' feet.

After this special Passover meal (which we now celebrate as Holy Communion), Jesus went to the garden of Gethsemane at the foot of the Mount of Olives, and He asked His friends to keep watch and pray with Him. Despite the torment Jesus knew the next few hours would bring for Him, He still prayed for His friends and instructed them to pray for themselves.

> At last he stood up again and returned to the disciples, only to find them asleep, exhausted from grief. "Why are you sleeping?" he asked them. "Get up and pray, so that you will not give in to temptation."
>
> (Luke 22:45–46)

We know from previous chapters Jesus used this time to specifically pray to God concerning His heart and mind—that He did not want to continue with the unfolding of this plan. However, His love for us and His Father superseded His momentary weakness, and He ended His prayers by asking for God's will to be done.

> "Abba, Father," he cried out, "everything is possible for you. Please take this cup of suffering away from me. Yet I want your will to be done, not mine."
>
> (Mark 14:36)

Later, when the soldiers converged on the garden, a few of the disciples readied themselves for a fight, and one even cut off the ear of the high priest's servant with a sword. Did Jesus ask them to fight and defend Him? No. He did the opposite. Even amid His personal turmoil, Jesus called for peace and responded with healing.

> But Jesus answered, "No more of this!" And he touched

the man's ear and healed him.

(Luke 22:51)

From here, we know the ugliness with which this story unfolds. As physical blow upon blow landed upon the Savior's fragile human form, and as insults and jeers cascaded like rain, not once did Jesus fight back, resort to anger, or ask for retribution. Even in these agonizing moments, Jesus continued to pray for others, including offering forgiveness to His enemies, even as they nailed Him to the cross.

> Jesus said, "Father, forgive them, for they don't know what they are doing." And the soldiers gambled for his clothes by throwing dice.

(Luke 23:34)

Jesus maintained insurmountable courage and steadfastness in the face of fear and the tremendous physical pain of crucifixion. In the midst of all this, He reached out to the criminal hanging next to Him and offered him reassurance and salvation. The man said:

> "We deserve to die for our crimes, but this man hasn't done anything wrong." Then he said, "Jesus, remember me when you come into your Kingdom."

> And Jesus replied, "I assure you, today you will be with me in paradise."

(Luke 23:41–43)

Three hours later, Jesus confidently gave up His spirit to God and was reunited with Him.

Then Jesus shouted, "Father, I entrust my spirit into your hands!"

And with those words he breathed his last.

(Luke 23:46)

What have we learned from how Jesus handled death? We know to find comfort in religious tradition, to serve others, to gather in fellowship, to find opportunities to teach, to pray for and with others and for ourselves, to continue to offer the good news of salvation up until our last breath, and to let go of this body and this world confidently with the expectation of entering into eternity with our Heavenly Father.

All of this makes great sense if we know in some way our time is drawing near, but we may not realistically have that knowledge. Does it truly matter, though? If we know that each day we live is also a day closer to death, why do we live as if death will never come, rather than living each day as if it were our last? Why do we not "take care of business" like we know we should? I say, mend those fences, offer forgiveness, and pray for the courage to follow God's

> *If we know that each day we live is also a day closer to death, why do we live as if death will never come, rather than living each day as if it were our last?*

will even when it's hard. Decide if (in my son's words) we want to get buried or burned. Do the hard and good work of preparation. Spread the news of salvation to every person we encounter.

After striving to live our lives like Jesus inside and out, may we approach the end of our time on earth with the certainty of our impending reunion with our glorious Savior in heaven. May we follow the example of Jesus, even unto death.

LIVE LIKE JESUS

Inside . . .

Walking through Jesus's last hours on earth offers insight into how we, too, can approach death. In His last moments, Jesus didn't abandon the way He'd lived His life; instead, He used every last opportunity to continue living as He always had—by serving God.

. . . and Out

Think about ways you can spend whatever time you have left in this world living like Jesus, inside and out.

Acknowledgements

I want to thank my husband and children first, because their lives are book fodder, and they love and support me despite this fact. Thanks for doing the dishes, acting as my constant sounding board, and eating takeout because I was wrapped up in the making of this book.

I am eternally grateful to my beta readers: Jerry and Caroline Dechert, Kristi Giles, Jan Faught, Melissa Reasoner, Andy Magee, Keri Wilt, Steven Kensing, Renee Bolton, and John Carlson. I could not have done this without you. Thank you for eating the "test pancake."

Ambra Starr Harrah, your support and encouragement make me a better person in every way, and the book blurb interview was pivotal.

To my prayer warrior and the best cheerleader around, Nancy Freedle, only heaven knows the disasters you've prevented on my behalf. Thank you for being my Aaron and Hur.

Everyone needs a friend who helps her see herself in a new light. Leah Westra, you taught me I can be many things simultaneously: a career woman, a published writer, and a woman of God. Thank you for your guidance and for believing in me.

My Thursday morning Woman-to-Woman Bible study ladies, I'm so grateful for your love, prayers, and encouragement. Thanks for allowing this "youngster" to join your group. Andy, I am forever grateful for your invitations and support.

To my team at Xulon Press, and especially to Kim Small and my editor, Friederich Schulte, thank you for helping me send these thoughts into the world. May God get all the glory for the work we do on His behalf.

Endnotes

1   Kristi McLelland, The Gospel on the Ground, (Brentwood: Lifeway Press, 2022), 145.

2   Billy Graham. "Five verses on hope found in Jesus Christ." billygrahamlibrary.org. Accessed September 1, 2023. https://billygrahamlibrary.org/5-verses-on-hope-found-in-jesus-christ/.

3   Henri J. M. Nouwen. "Here and Now: Living in the Spirit." goodreads.com. Accessed September 1, 2023. https://www.goodreads.com/work/quotes/140495-here-and-now-living-in-the-spirit.

4   Tim Keller. Instagram quote. December 16, 2023. https://www.instagram.com/p/C07yAC2ROUa/.

5   Epictetus. "Epictetus quotes." BrainyQuote. Accessed February 6, 2022. https://www.brainyquote.com/authors/epictetus-quotes.

6   Tony Evans. Instagram post. January 29, 2024. https://www.instagram.com/p/C2sSiUcukYY/.

7   Nicki Dechert Carlson. Grace-Faced: Pursuing the Life-Changing Perspective of a Loving God (Maitland: Xulon Press, 2021), 10.

8   Koinonia House, "Thank You For The Fleas," November 24, 2009, https://www.khouse.org/enews_article/2009/1544/print/.

9   Rick Warren, The Purpose-Driven Life, (Grand Rapids: Zondervan, 2002), 148.

10   Dr. Constance Cherry, Worship like Jesus, worshipleader.com, May 4, 2020, https://worshipleader.com/leadership/worship-like-jesus/.

11 Kristi McLelland, The Gospel on the Ground (Brentwood: Lifeway Press, 2022), 78.

12 Stan Mitchell. Instagram post. May 20, 2020. https://www. instagram.com/p/CAbvVo6BVn6/.

13 Compassion International. "Definition and Understanding the Meaning of Mercy." Accessed November 29, 2023. https://www. compassion.com/poverty/mercy-definition.htm.

14 Henri Nouwen. "Henri J.M. Nouwen quotes." goodreads.com. Accessed February 16, 2024. https://www.goodreads.com/author/ quotes/4837.Henri_J_M_Nouwen.

15 Lukas Lezon. Lukelezon Instagram post. November 5, 2017.

16 Carlos A. Rodriguez. thehappygivers Instagram post. March 7, 2023. https://www.instagram.com/p/CpgHOitvtPL/.

17 Nicki Dechert Carlson. Grace-Faced: Pursuing the Life-Changing Perspective of a Loving God (Maitland: Xulon Press, 2021), 80.

18 Julian of Norwich. Julian of Norwich. "Julian of Norwich quotes." A-Z Quotes. Accessed February 17, 2024. https://www.azquotes. com/author/17697-Julian_of_Norwich/tag/prayer.

19 Gema Sánchez Cuevas. "Socrates' Triple Filter Test." Exploring Your Mind. Accessed February 18, 2024. https://exploringyourmind. com/socrates-triple-filter-test/.

20 Fred (Mister) Rogers. "64 Mister Rogers Quotes That Will Make Today a Beautiful Day." Parade. Accessed August 5, 2021. https:// parade.com/954616/alexandra-hurtado/mr-rogers-quotes/.